Management of
Dementia

Department of Social Policy and Social Work
University of Oxford
Barnett House
32 Wellington Square
Oxford OX1 2ER
England

Management of Dementia

Simon Lovestone, *Mphil MRCPsych PhD*
Professor of Old Age Psychiatry
Departments of Old Age Psychiatry and Neuroscience
Institute of Psychiatry
London, UK
Serge Gauthier, *MD FRCPC*
Professor and Director
Alzheimer's Disease Research Unit
The McGill Centre for Studies in Aging
Douglas Hospital
Verdun PQ, Canada

MARTIN DUNITZ

© Martin Dunitz Ltd 2001

First published in the United Kingdom in 2001 by
Martin Dunitz Ltd
The Livery House
7–9 Pratt Street
London NW1 0AE

Tel: +44-(0)20-7482-2202
Fax: +44-(0)20-7267-0159
E-mail: info.dunitz@tandf.co.uk
Website: http://www.dunitz.co.uk

A CIP catalogue record for this book is available from the British Library

ISBN 1-85317-739-3

Composition by Wearset, Boldon, Tyne and Wear
Printed and bound in Italy by Printer Trento

Contents

Simon Lovestone is Professor of Old Age Psychiatry at the Institute of Psychiatry, King's College Hospital. After working as a junior doctor in medicine and in health care of the elderly he trained in psychiatry and then obtained a Wellcome Trust fellowship to study the molecular relationship between plaques and tangles. After obtaining an MPhil in Psychiatry and a PhD in biochemistry, he became Senior Lecturer and then Reader in Old Age Psychiatry and Neuroscience before becoming Professor at the Institute and consultant Old Age Psychiatrist at the Maudsley hospital.

Serge Gauthier graduated from Université de Montréal's Medical School in 1973 and McGill University Neurology Training Program in 1976. After two years of Neurochemistry training with Professor Theodore Sourkes at the Allan Memorial Insititute, he was Full Time Geographic at the Montreal Neurological Institute. From 1986 to 1996 he was Director of the McGill Centre for Studies in Aging and is currently recipient of a Research Chair from the Medical Research Council of Canada, and Director of the Alzheimer Disease Research Unit of the McGill Centre for Studies in Aging.

Preface

This is an important time for Alzheimer's disease. Almost 100 years after Alzheimer published his case we are approaching what feels like the end game. Within the last decade Alzheimer's disease has gone from a largely ignored and poorly understood backwater of neurology and psychiatry to the mainstream. Public recognition of the disorder grows apace, partly as a result of the growing media exposure in turn resulting from the admirable openness of many sufferers and their carers and partly as a result of the growing strength of the lay societies. The medical disciplines caring for those with dementia – old age psychiatry, neurology, geriatric medicine – grow in confidence and 'dementia-ology' is no longer the Cinderella specialism it was. Other professionals from nursing, psychology and occupational therapy through to social work, speech therapy, even our colleagues in complimentary medicine – aromatherapists and others – are all taking a special interest in dementia. Scientists became interested again in AD in the 1960s and 1970s and the fruits of the labours of the neurochemists and neuropathologists are the first specific drugs for the disorder which reached patients in the late 1990s. Now the geneticists and the molecular biologists are in full swing and the hope is that the result of this latest wave in research will be treatments that might delay, prevent or even cure this terrible, cursed disorder.

In this book we have tried to do two things – to selectively review the current state of knowledge, and to distil some of our personal experience of dementia care. In writing we have had a particular reader in mind – he or she is working in dementia care and wants to practice evidence-based medicine without losing sight of the person receiving care. He or she wants to use the best, most appropriate pharmacology whilst also using other non-pharmacological treatments often and appropriately. He or she wants to be able to work with carers whether offering genetic advice or helping to run a carer support group. He or she is very like ourselves.

We have tried to cover some of the issues we find both most difficult and most interesting as well as those most important to patients and carers. Often these are the same issues. In Chapter 1 we consider issues such as whom to tell and how to discuss prognosis, in Chapter 2 the differences between psychiatric symptoms and behavioural disturbance are discussed; in Chapter 3 we face one of the

problems most distressing to relatives and one we find hardest to treat – sleep disturbance. In Chapter 4 we consider the management of depression and other psychiatric symptoms, and in Chapter 5 we discuss some issues of direct clinical relevance that result from the new molecular medicine of Alzheimer's disease. In Chapter 6 the disease-specific cholinesterase inhibitors are reviewed, but neurotransmitter therapies in AD go beyond modulating the cholinergic system as we consider in Chapter 7. We allow ourselves a little future-gazing in Chapter 8 when we consider therapies that might modify the disease process in the future. In Chapter 9, we consider longer-term and respite care for dementia patients. Finally we consider some specific scenarios in algorithms for treatment and include also some of the scales for assessment we find most useful in clinical practice.

We hope that this small book is a useful contribution to your practical management of Alzheimer's disease.

Simon Lovestone
Serge Gauthier

Managing the newly diagnosed patient

1

Discussing the diagnosis with patients and carers

In the context of dementia, a number of guidelines (Post and Whitehouse, 1995), task forces (Fisk et al, 1998) and surveys (Boise et al, 1999) have confirmed that the patient has the right to receive a specific diagnosis, unless he or she waives it. But in practice there are a number of issues that require flexibility from the physician responsible for disclosure (Johnson et al, 2000). This chapter will outline some of the issues and offer practical solutions, the guiding principle being to give an honest presentation of information as it is perceived and known at the different stages of the assessment process (Drickamer and Lachs, 1992).

Should diagnosis of dementia be made early?

Clearly yes, to clarify uncertainty about the nature of symptoms ranging from apathy and social withdrawal to mistakes in handling routine tasks at home or at work. Concomitant disorders such as depression and hypothyroidism can also be treated, giving the opportunity to plan for the future. Symptomatic drugs can be offered and stabilisation treatments are under study.

Is there enough certainty about the clinical diagnosis of dementia and its specific causes?

Yes, if one takes the appropriate steps of history taking with patient and informant, physical examination, mental status assessment, relevant laboratory tests and follow-up over time until the requirements of the DSM-IV for dementia are met (Panel 1.1).

The specific cause of dementia can often be positively identified from the pattern of symptoms as illustrated in Figure 1.1 for the typical patient with Alzheimer's disease (AD). The initial and transient change in mood is followed by a linear decline in cognitive and functional abilities, then disruptive neuropsychiatric symptoms emerge and abate, followed by progressive rigidity, akinesia and gait instability. Each of the less common type of dementia has its own set of diagnostic criteria (Panels 1.2, 1.3 and 1.4). Of particular significance are the delirium-like fluctuating confusion and visual hallucinations in dementia with Lewy bodies (DLB; McKeith, 2000), the early loss of personal and social awareness combined with reduction in speech associated with fronto-temporal dementia (Mann et al, 2000), and the stepwise deterioration with asymmetric neurological signs in vascular dementia (Erkinjuntti and Pantoni, 2000).

Panel 1.1
Diagnostic criteria for dementia of the Alzheimer's type

Multiple cognitive deficits
- *in memory*
- *one or more of language, praxis, gnosis, executive functioning*

Causing
- *significant impairment and decline in social or occupational functioning*
- *gradual onset and continuing cognitive decline*

Not due to
- *other central nervous system or substance-induced conditions*
- *deficits not exclusively during course of delirium and not better accounted for by depression or schizophrenia*

*Modified from American Psychiatric Association, 1994.

Panel 1.2
Diagnostic criteria for dementia with Lewy bodies

*Progressive cognitive decline interfering with social or occupational functioning
One (possible DLB) or two (probable DLB) of:*
- *fluctuating cognition with pronounced variations*
- *recurrent visual hallucinations*
- *spontaneous motor features of Parkinsonism*

*Modified from McKeith et al, 1996.

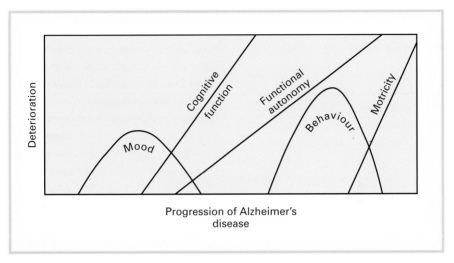

Progression of Alzheimer's
disease

Figure 1
Pattern of symptoms over time in typical patients with Alzheimer's disease.

Panel 1.3
Diagnostic criteria for fronto-temporal dementia

- *behavioural disturbances, including early loss of personal and social awareness*
- *affective symptoms, including emotional unconcern*
- *speech disorder, including reduction, stereotypy, and perseveration*
- *physical signs, including primitive reflexes, incontinence, akinesia, and rigidity*

*Modified from Lund Manchester Groups, 1994.

Panel 1.4
Diagnostic criteria for vascular dementia*

- *decline in intellectual function sufficient to interfere with activities of daily life and not due to the physical effects of stroke(s) alone*
- *evidence by history, physical, and/or neuroimaging examination of stroke(s)*
- *temporal relationship between dementia and cerebrovascular disease*

*Modified from Chui et al, 1993, and Roman et al, 1994.

Is there a differential approach for telling patients with different types of dementia about their diagnosis?

Yes. Most people dislike the term 'dementia' because it has the connotation of mental illness, thus patients and carers will prefer a 'disease' label. Using a good news/bad news approach, people are often reassured by the knowledge that there is a specific cause for the symptoms, and that specific drugs can be tried to control them. The lack of known genetic risk for children of patients with DLB may offer some relief (but this is not the case for AD, see Chapter 5). The relatively stable course of vascular dementia compared to AD (at least in the short term) may also offer some additional hope.

Is there a right time to give the diagnosis?

As clinicians we may suspect that a patient is progressing towards a dementia such as AD long before the symptoms reach diagnostic threshold. For instance, a long postoperative delirium could antedate AD by a number of years. A decline on serial Mini Mental State Examination scores could precede symptoms (Small et al, 2000). The converse is also true, where families detect changes in mood, personality, and initiative that they have seen associated with dementia in older relatives. If in doubt about the presence of dementia, it is better to state that it is not present at this time,

but that follow-up is required once a year, with attention to risk factors such as systolic hypertension. This may be a good time to 'put the papers in order' such as will and advance directives, when people are fully competent to do so, and identify who is likely to be the most significant family member to act as carer, should the need arise. Once the diagnosis of dementia is clear in the clinician's mind and documented in his chart, this carer should be notified without delay. If the patient is in an angry denial stage, it may be better to give him or her disclosure in a stepwise approach. Once insight into the significance of dementia has been lost in intermediate to late stages, there should be no hesitation about keeping the patient informed, in clear but truthful language.

Should we tell a patient with mild cognitive impairment that they may progress to dementia?

Yes, with the reassuring news that most persons with mild cognitive impairment as currently defined (Panel 1.5) do not progress to AD. Since up to 15% a year do progress to AD (Petersen et al, 1999), interested patients can be referred to research sites running one of the many studies in this population.

Assessment of care needs

As a component of history taking towards the diagnosis of dementia, the clinician will have

Panel 1.5
*Operational definition of mild cognitive impairment**

* *subjective memory complaints*
* *abnormal memory tests for age and level of education*
* *normal general cognitive performance*
* *normal activities of daily living*
* *not demented clinically*

*Petersen et al, 1999.

acquired knowledge of the functional abilities of the individual, and of the resources available to cope with difficulties. For instance, someone may already be helping with finances and transportation. As part of a management strategy, additional information should be obtained on the person's life story, including work and leisure activities, as well as the quality of their social network, including family and close friends. Special attention will have to be paid to the carer, especially if older and frail, but also to a daughter or son caught between their responsibilities towards an elderly parent and their own children and spouse (the 'sandwich' effect). Family therapy or individual treatment for the distressed carer may be needed (Dunkin and Anderson-Hanley, 1998).

Referral to a local Alzheimer society, whatever the cause of dementia, is an important step in the education of patients and carers (Maheu and Cohen, 2001).

Referral to local community-based formal support services for help at home and access to support groups, day programmes, and respite care is another useful step, often underused by families (Katofsky and Levin, 2001).

Prognosis

The natural history of AD can be understood as a series of milestones that can be used in clinical trials as outcome, or in patients' and caregivers' education (Gauthier, 2000; Panel 1.6).

There have been many attempts to predict which patients will do better or worse (Panisset and Stern, 2001). A list derived from many publications for clinical features that predict a rapid decline is shown in Panel 1.7.

The clinician will have to schedule closer visits on follow-up of patients in the rapid-

Panel 1.6
*Milestones in progression of dementia**

* *conversion from mild cognitive impairment to dementia*
* *loss of instrumental activities of daily living (ADL)*
* *emergence of neuropsychiatric symptoms*
* *nursing-home placement*
* *loss of self-care ADLs*
* *death*

*Gauthier, 2000.

Panel 1.7
Clinical features suggestive of rapid decline

- *aphasia, severe*
- *caregiver psychological morbidity*
- *concomitant vascular disease*
- *extra-pyramidal signs, early*
- *greater age*
- *myoclonus, early*
- *non-AD dementias*
- *psychosis, early*
- *unmarried men*

Referral to specialist services

Although family practitioners have a central role in the diagnosis and management of dementia (Downs, 1996), they will face uncertainty in some patients with very early symptoms, atypical presentations of AD, or rare types of dementia. Some of the management issues need a team approach, both in the community and in institutions. Guidelines have been prepared to suggest when to refer to a specialist (Panel 1.8).

decline category, give advance warning of things to come, and facilitate planning for the carer, all the way to nursing-home placement. An example of how such cases may pan out follows. A woman practicing family medicine in her mid-fifties is brought to her physician by her husband because of mistakes at work over the past year. She has significant difficulties expressing herself in her second language and is reverting to her mother tongue, not well understood by the spouse. Myoclonus is visible in her limbs. The diagnosis of AD is made, confirmed by consultation with a specialist, and the spouse is warned of the poor prognosis. There was no improvement on a cholinesterase inhibitor, and she needed nursing-home placement 1 year later. The spouse had taken a year off work to care for her at home, and was able to go back to teaching. She died a year later from pneumonia.

Panel 1.8
Reasons to consider referral to a specialist

- *continuing uncertainty about the diagnosis after initial assessment and follow-up*
- *request by family or patient for second opinion*
- *presence of significant not responsive to treatment*
- *intolerance or lack of response to disease-specific pharmacotherapy*
- *need for additional help for patient management or caregiver support*
- *need to involve other health professionals, voluntary agencies, or local service providers*
- *when genetic counselling is indicated*
- *when research studies into diagnosis or treatment are being carried out*

Patterson et al, 1999.

Summary

- Family practitioners play a key role in the diagnosis and management of people with dementia and their carers.

- Practitioners have responsibility for disclosure of diagnosis, assessment of care needs, and prognosis.

- Carers and practitioners can and should call upon a number of resources in their community.

References

American Psychiatric Association (1994). *Diagnosis and statistical manual of mental disorders*, 4th edn. Washington DC: APA.

Boise L, Morgan DL, Kaye J, Camicioli R (1999). Delays in the diagnosis of dementia: perspectives of family caregivers. *Am J Alzheimer Dis* 1, 20–26.

Chui HC, Victoroff JI, Margolin D et al (1993). Criteria for the diagnosis of ischemic vascular dementia proposed by the State of California Alzheimer's Disease Diagnostic and Treatment Centres. *Neurology* 42, 473–80.

Downs MG (1996). The role of general practice and the primary care team in dementia diagnosis and management. *Int J Geriatr Psychiatry* 11, 937–42.

Drickamer MA, Lachs MS (1992). Should patients with Alzheimer's disease be told of their diagnosis? *N Engl J Med* 326, 947–51.

Dunkin JJ, Anderson-Hanley C (1998). Dementia caregiver burden: a review of the literature and guidelines for assessment and intervention. *Neurology* 51, S53–S60.

Erkinjuntti T, Pantoni L (2000). Subcortical vascular dementia. In: Gauthier S, Cummings JL, eds. *Alzheimer's disease and related disorders annual*. London: Martin Dunitz, 101–34.

Fisk JD, Sadovnick AD, Cohen CA, et al (1998). Ethical guidelines of the Alzheimer Society of Canada. *Can J Neurol Sci* 25, 242–48.

Gauthier S (2000). Impact of new therapies on the management of Alzheimer's disease. *Int Med J* 7, 3–6.

Johnson H, Bouman WP, Pinner G (2000). On telling the truth in Alzheimer's disease: a pilot study of current practice and attitudes. *Int Psychogeriatrics* 12, 221–29.

Katofsky L, Dulka IM (2001). Community-based formal support services. In: Gauthier S, ed. *Clinical diagnosis and management of Alzheimer's disease*. London: Martin Dunitz, 2nd rev edn, 319–32.

Lund and Manchester Groups (1994). Clinical and neuropathological criteria for fronto-temporal dementia. *J Neurol Neurosurg Psychiatry* 57, 416–18.

Maheu S, Cohen CA (2001). Support of families. In: Gauthier S, ed. *Clinical diagnosis and management of Alzheimer's disease*. London: Martin Dunitz, 2nd rev edn, 307–18.

Mann D, Neary D, Snowden JS (2000). Chromosome 17 and frontotemporal dementia. In: Gauthier S, Cummings JL, eds. *Alzheimer's disease and related disorders annual*. London: Martin Dunitz, 27–56.

McKeith I (2000). Dementia with Lewy bodies. In: Gauthier S, Cummings JL, eds. *Alzheimer's disease and related disorders annual*. London: Martin Dunitz, 57–76.

McKeith IG, Galasko D, Kosaka K, et al (1996). Consensus guidelines for the clinical and pathological diagnosis of dementia with Lewy bodies (DLB): report of the consortium on

DLB international workshop. *Neurology* 47, 1113–24.

Panisset M, Stern Y (2001). Prognostic factors. In: Gauthier S, ed. *Clinical diagnosis and management of Alzheimer's disease.* London: Martin Dunitz, 2nd rev edn, 157–66.

Patterson C, Gauthier S, Bergman H, et al (1999). The recognition, assessment and management of dementing disorders: conclusions from the Canadian Consensus Conference on Dementia. *CMAJ* 160 (suppl), S1–S20.

Petersen RC, Smith GE, Waring SC, Ivnik RJ, Tangalos EG, Kohmen E (1999). Mild cognitive impairment: clinical characterization and outcome. *Arch Neurol* 56, 303–8.

Post SG, Whitehouse PJ (1995). Fairhill guidelines on ethics of the care of people with Alzheimer's disease: a clinical summary. *J Am Ger Soc* 43, 1423–29.

Roman GC, Tatemichi TK, Erkinjuntii T, et al (1994). Vascular dementia: diagnostic criteria for research studies: report of the NINCDS-AIREN international workshop. *Neurology* 43, 250–60.

Small BJ, Fratiglioni L, Viitanen M, Winblad B, Bäckman L (2000). The course of cognitive impairment in preclinical Alzheimer's disease. *Arch Neurol* 57, 839–44.

Behavioural disturbance

2

What is behavioural disturbance?

The range of symptoms of Alzheimer's disease (AD) often comes as a surprise to those encountering it for the first time. Perhaps it should not; Alzheimer's first reported case was of a woman suffering not only the characteristic memory impairment but also what are now thought of as non-cognitive neuropsychiatric symptoms or behavioural complications. Not all of these symptoms result in behavioural disturbance, because many patients experience some neuropsychiatric symptoms that can be determined by close examination but have no discernible disturbed behaviour. Equally, behavioural disturbance can arise without any detectable neuropsychiatric symptomatology. Behavioural disturbance, for the purposes of practical management and this chapter, is any behaviour exhibited by the patient with AD that gives rise to concern either for the patient, the carers, or, conceivably, for others. Defined in this way, behavioural disturbance is a partly subjective set that overlaps with, but does not exactly coincide with, the set of non-cognitive symptoms or behavioural complications described in AD and measured by various scales. Not surprisingly, given this third-person-based definition, the assessment of behavioural disturbance is dependant on the caregiver and may differ between family and professional carers (Lukovits and McDaniel, 1992). Most importantly, it is appropriate to distinguish between behavioural disturbance and psychiatric phenomena, because the management of behavioural disturbance requires a different set of responses to that for management of neuropsychiatric symptoms.

Behavioural disturbance includes behaviours such as wandering, aggression, abnormal eating, apathy, agitation, disinhibition, incontinence, and other behaviours likely to give rise to difficulties for the patient or others. Some of these behavioural disturbances are common, others less so, but all change with the disease itself, becoming more or less troublesome as the disease progresses. Assessment of the frequency of behavioural disturbance in AD is therefore a challenge, particularly because whether a behaviour is disturbed or not depends on the observer and the environment the patient is in. However, studies of mild (Wild et al, 1994) and moderately (Teri et al, 1989) demented patients show that behavioural disturbance starts early in the disease process and may bear little consistent relation to severity. Psychosis and agitation, for example, can both occur early (Jost and Grossberg, 1996; Mortimer et al, 1992). Longitudinal studies suggest that the various behaviours that cause disturbance may have a different relation to severity. Apathy, for example, may be more closely linked to the

severity of the condition than other behaviours (Marin et al, 1997). It is apparent, however, that although behaviour disturbance changes with the natural progression of AD, many factors make a greater contribution to whether disturbed behaviour is present than the cognitive impairment itself (Cooper et al, 1990). Other behaviours such as incontinence are almost entirely a feature of advanced disease, when they are so common as to be almost ubiquitous. Other behaviours are uncommon, such as shoplifting, or almost unique to individual patients such as the elderly woman referred because she painted mirrors – a result of the disturbing symptom of failing to recognise her own reflection (autoprosopagnosia).

The following types of behavioural disturbance are recognised:

- wandering: wandering out of the house/home; following carers; wandering in the house/home
- aggression: verbal; physical
- abnormal eating: anorexia; bulimia; pica (eating non-food stuffs); change in tastes
- apathy
- agitation: hand wringing; pacing; anxiety
- disinhibition: sexual disinhibition
- vocalisations: moaning; screaming

Causes of behavioural disturbance

Given that behavioural disturbance is a complex interplay between the patient, symptoms, and response of those caring for them there is unlikely to be a simple 'cause' of behavioural disturbance. To take just one example – aggression – understanding can be sought at a neurobiological, clinical, or environmental level. Thus specific neuronal loss is reported in aggression in AD (Forstl et al, 1994) and altered adrenergic function could affect aggression; one study suggests that alpha-2 adrenergic receptors are increased in aggressive AD patients at post mortem relative to patients without aggression (Russo-Neustadt and Cotman, 1997). At a clinical level, aggression has been shown to correlate very highly with psychosis (Aarsland et al, 1996) and the presence of delusions are the best clinical indicator for occurrence of aggressive features (Gilley et al, 1997; Gormley et al, 1998). However, it is also true that aggression in patients is frequently in response to some other event – a carer trying to help the patient to dress or admission to a new day-centre, for example. Similarly, changes in levels of apathy or agitation may be due to selective neuronal loss, to an underlying depression, or to an external cause such as a change in carer or physical illness (Mintzer and Brawman Mintzer, 1996).

For practical management purposes it can be helpful to categorise behavioural disturbance in relation to physical factors, to activities of daily living and care tasks, and to time of day; when there is no apparent relation to other factors this should also be noted, as well as secondary relations to neuropsychiatric symptoms. A mnemonic can help professional carers, who are paid to manage behavioural disturbance, to recall these categories. Assessment of patients by the PAID approach (Physical, Activity-related, Intrinsic, Depression and Delusions) can assist management (see panel 2.1). So, for example the management of a patient aggressive only when being helped to dress is quite different from the management of an aggressive patient who also has psychotic symptoms. Similarly, the management of a patient who wanders towards evening is different from the

Panel 2.1
Determining the 'cause' of behavioural and psychological symptoms of dementia (BPSD) – the PAID approach

> *BPSD may be:*
> *secondary to **P**hysical problems*
> *related to **A**ctivity*
> ***I**ntrinsic to the disease*
> *as a consequence of **D**epression or delusion*
> *for example aggression can be associated with . . .*
>
> *Physical:*   *pain, infection, CCF*
> *Activity:*   *getting dressed, new carer*
> *Instrinsic:*   *personality change*
> *Delusions:*   *of theft, fear, hallucinations*

management of a patient who wanders throughout the day.

Physical causes of behavioural disturbance

Physical causes of behavioural disturbance are legion and multiple pathologies are common in the elderly. Infection resulting in a delirium, or more frequently a sub-acute confusional state, can give rise to behavioural disturbance and should be suspected if the behavioural disturbance is of sudden onset or coincides with other symptoms. Heart failure or chest disease resulting in a mild anoxic state also increases confusion. Chronic pain is distressing, but for those with dementia must be even more so, and if there is external evidence of arthritis or another potential cause of pain then a course of analgesia can be a useful approach for behavioural disturbance. Careful attention should be paid to medication and potential drug interactions; in those receiving poly-pharmacy an initial approach to behavioural disturbance can be to reduce, and stop, all but the most essential drugs.

Activity-related behavioural disturbance

Although there is no empirical evidence to support the claim, clinical experience suggests that most behavioural disturbance is related to an activity of some sort. Some patients become disturbed only when the carer attempts to dress them or to engage them in some other activity. Professional carers develop working relationships with patients and a change in carer can result in a change in behaviour that is interpreted by the new carer as disturbed. Similarly, a move to a day centre, admission to hospital, or the transition to continuing care can all result in behavioural disturbance that may be of short duration only.

Intrinsic behavioural disturbances

Some behaviours appear to bear no relation to physical, environmental, or neuropsychiatric events. Wandering, picking behaviours, and changes in eating habits all fall into this category. Whether these changes in behaviour amount to disturbance depends upon the extent of the behaviour and responses of others. Take wandering, for example: one patient of ours wanders frequently in the local streets around her home, which in an inner-city environment is a risky activity, but this is tolerated by her carers and she is often returned home by neighbours. Another patient wanders inside his home, never attempting to leave and putting himself in no danger, but this, however, causes intense distress to his spouse-carer making the wandering a target behaviour necessitating treatment. Changes in circadian rhythms with increasing confusion towards the end of the day (sun-downing) or decreased sleep at night occur frequently in AD and this can result in behavioural disturbance. Almost any activity at night can amount to behavioural disturbance and can result in disproportionate stress to carers. Behavioural disturbance towards the evening is often a sign of increased confusion.

Depression and delusions: neuropsychiatric causes of behavioural disturbance

In scales designed to assess the non-cognitive symptomatology of AD, neuropsychiatric symptoms and behavioural disturbances are often conflated for convenience, although as we stress in this chapter not all behavioural disturbances result from neuropsychiatric symptoms. Nonetheless, the most robust empirical evidence on the cause of behavioural disturbances links aggression to psychotic phenomena. Psychosis, particularly delusions, are the best clinical indicator of aggressive behaviour (Aarsland et al, 1996; Gilley et al, 1997; Gormley et al, 1998). The reason why psychotic symptoms result in disturbed behaviour is not known. Experience of individual patients with psychosis and dementia suggests that sometimes the experiences result directly in a disturbed behaviour – throwing stones at hallucinatory intruders in the garden or shouting at voices

are two examples that come to mind. On other occasions it can be difficult to discern any direct relation between the psychosis and the disturbed behaviour, although even a cursory attempt at empathizing with the experience must come to the conclusion that while any delusion or hallucination must be unpleasant, to have such an experience in the context of confusion must be highly disturbing.

Core symptoms of depression include changes of activity such as apathy or agitation and these may be the only manifestation of mood disorder in patients with dementia. Mania can always result in extremely disruptive behaviour but when it occurs as part of a dementia is both easy to confuse with other syndromes and difficult to treat.

Assessment

Assessment starts with a careful history from an informant. The nature and natural history of the behavioural disturbance is noted. When did it start, has it got worse, exactly what occurs? Most importantly, the relation between the behavioural disturbance and activities or recent events should be sought. Does the behavioural disturbance only occur when the patient is interacting with another? Did it first start when the patient was admitted to a home? What steps have been taken so far and has there been any change? It is critical to establish the recent health of the patient, and any medication currently or recently taken. The examination should include an observation of the behaviour wherever possible (although this is surprisingly often difficult to achieve) and assessment of the environment before a physical examination for concurrent illness and a psychiatric examination for signs of psychotic or affective disorder. Investigations should include a screen for physical illness, especially infection. The key to good management is accurate assessment and a systematic approach, such as PAID.

Instruments have been developed to assess behavioural disturbance and neuropsychiatric symptoms objectively and reliably; these have enabled research on the causes, effects, and management of symptoms and also have an important role in clinical practice, particularly in specialist multidisciplinary care. Standardised behaviour scales not only measure change reliably but also enable different members of the team to have a commonly agreed baseline assessment on which to build specialist assessments appropriate to their various disciplines. However, many of these scales and instruments conflate behavioural and neuropsychiatric symptoms and so in clinical use a careful judgement of impact of the different symptoms or categories of the symptoms must be made. One of the most widely used scales, the Behavioural Pathology in Alzheimer's Disease (BEHAVE-AD) rating

scale (Reisberg et al, 1987), has, for example, categories such as paranoia and delusions, hallucinations, activity, aggression, sleep disturbance, mood, and anxiety. Some of these categories are very likely to result in behavioural disturbance, others less so. All categories, of course, may or may not require appropriate management. Other scales more consciously assess those elements that are likely to impact upon carers, such as the Behaviour and Mood Disturbance scale (Greene et al, 1982), while others assess specific behaviours. The behaviours that often cause carer difficulties include agitation and aggression; scales for both have been developed. Agitation is assessed in a nurse-rated scale by the Cohen-Mansfield Agitation Inventory (Cohen-Mansfield, 1986) although doubts have been raised as to the inter-rater reliability of some aspects of the scale (Finkel et al, 1992). Aggression is measured specifically by the Rating of Aggressive Behaviour in the elderly (RAGE; Patel and Hope, 1992). The Disruptive Behavior Rating Scales (DBRS), covering both agitation and aggression as well as wandering, is based on a checklist format completed by nursing staff and was designed originally for use in nursing homes (Mungas et al, 1989). Perhaps the most complete assessment instrument, however, is a semi-structured interview with carers – the Present Behavioural Examination (PBE; Hope and Fairburn, 1992), although completing the assessment is time-consuming.

Which of these instruments is chosen depends on the context – the location of the patient, the availability of carers or professional staff, the time available for assessment, and, most importantly, the purpose of the assessment. For example, a study to detect the impact of a new drug on non-cognitive symptoms without a hypothesis on which symptom is most likely to be affected may choose to use BEHAVE-AD. By contrast, to examine specific behaviours it is preferable to use a designated scale; for example in a study of psychosis and aggression RAGE was a useful choice (Gormley et al, 1998). In clinical practice any of the scales mentioned here can be a useful addition to clinical assessment, especially to provide objective baseline assessments and a measure of change in response to an intervention.

Impact of disturbance

By definition behavioural disturbance is disruptive. In this chapter we use the term behavioural disturbance in the context of impact on carers and others. Many published papers point to the impact of dementia upon carers (see chapter 7) and attempts have been made to determine those aspects of dementia that are most distressing. Some studies have suggested that disturbed behaviour, variously defined, has a greater impact than some other characteristics of patients (Coen et al, 1997; Zarit et al, 1986; Teri et al, 1992; Quayhagen

and Quayhagen, 1988; Pruchno and Resch, 1989). Partly because of the impact of behavioural disturbance on carers and partly because these behaviours often demand specialist care, one of the most important determinants of entry into institutionalised care is behavioural disturbance (Vernooij Dassen et al, 1997; Cohen et al, 1993). Behavioural disturbance is then a key target for intervention and this has been acknowledged in the design of drugs for use in AD where outcome measures routinely include not only the domains of cognition and function but also behaviour (Cummings, 1997). Changing behaviour seems to reduce carer burden (Bedard et al, 1997) – providing some hope that interventions will result in decreased impact of AD on others as well as on the patients themselves.

Management of behavioural disturbance

Specific interventions for neuropsychiatric complications, many of which result in behavioural disturbance, are discussed in chapter 4; here we consider management of behaviours such as agitation, wandering, and aggression – although, as noted above, the first step in management is accurate assessment treatment of any underlying cause of the behavioural disturbance (Forloni et al, 1997). For example, it goes without saying that if the agitation is because of inadequate analgesia for an arthritic knee, if the wandering is because of increased confusion secondary to concurrent infection or if underlying the aggression is a frank psychosis, then treatment should address these issues before any general management approach for behavioural disturbance.

General management approaches can be considered in three parts – behavioural, pharmacological, or institutional. Although one cannot be too proscriptive, these three approaches tend to be sequential (it is best first to attempt the intervention least likely to do harm) – the behavioural approach (which can be directed at either carer or patient), followed by judicious use of pharmacology, followed by entry into an institution. Appropriate use of institutional resources in respite or day care, however, can prevent premature full institutionalisation.

Behavioural management

Although probably the most used intervention in clinical practice, behavioural management of disrupted behaviours in AD has received only modest research attention (Maletta, 1988; Alessi, 1991). Nonetheless, non-pharmacological approaches are essential in the management of behavioural disturbance either as the only necessary intervention or as a supplement to drug treatments.

Reassessment of behaviour

Because behavioural disturbance results from the interaction between specific behaviours exhibited by patients and the responses of carers the first step is to work with the carers to reassess the behaviour. If carers can be helped to cope with or to contain a behaviour then although it may not cease to be a problem, it does at least become a manageable problem. Work with families and other carers has been shown to reduce carer stress (Mittelman et al, 1995) and almost certainly alters the perception of behaviours exhibited by the patient.

Case studies

An elderly man with mild dementia repeatedly asked his wife whether it was dinnertime soon. She, thinking this was the best approach, spent much of the day telling him the date, the time, and the weather and placed orientation boards in the living room and kitchen, just as she had seen in day-centres she had visited. Whenever he asked if it was nearly dinnertime she took him to one of the boards and tried to orientate him. This caused her to become frustrated and him to become agitated. The situation seemed to be escalating. To try to break the cycle the doctor in the team reassured her that it was unlikely that continual orientation practice would effect his disease progression and the community nurse persuaded her to remove both the orientation boards. She was encouraged to answer his question and to respond positively when he was correct or to carefully correct him when he was wrong. When he asked whether it was time for dinner it was suggested she reply 'soon, dear', 'quite a while, yet', or ask if he was hungry. He carried on asking but, since his wife had been relieved of the duty of re-orientating him, this repeated questioning became just a behaviour and not a disturbance.

In another example, the community team, over time, became aware that a particular nursing home was the source of a disproportionate number of referrals. These came to all members of the team and were for supposedly different behavioural disturbances. On reflection, however, it seemed that all of the referrals were for patients with advanced dementia who wandered within the home. The layout of the home was such that patients could not wander out of the building and, because the living areas were on different floors to the bedrooms, they rarely interfered with the privacy of other residents. A visit to the home and a short training period showed that a particularly conscientious manager thought that wandering was always a sign of some other problem. When it was explained that this was indeed sometimes the case but that patients with dementia sometimes wander for no apparent reason the manager and her staff were reassured and the patients were allowed to walk about the home, safely and without causing disturbance.

Changing behaviours by influencing the carer

While the perception of some behaviours can be changed from disturbed to acceptable with education, this is frequently not the case and the behaviour continues to be experienced as problematical. However, working with the carer to change the carer's behaviour can often result in a lessening either of the behaviour or a diminishing of its impact. The multi-disciplinary team has a key role in assessment of the behaviour of the patient, the immediate antecedent, and the response of carers. An intervention should be tailored to the individual carer and patient and designed either to remove the antecedents or to change the carer response. However, we find that one small intervention is more useful than almost any other – advising the carer to leave the patient for a short while if behavioural disturbance starts. Understandably carers are reluctant to leave a demented person especially if they are agitated or disturbed. However, when the behavioural disturbance results from an intervention made by the carer during a care task – washing or dressing, for example – this is often the only step needed to lessen the behavioural disturbance to manageable levels. We reassure the carer that so long as the patient is safe then walking away and returning a few minutes later is not only acceptable but of benefit to both, and that this simple act is sometimes the most important thing a dementia team can do.

Equally important but often harder to address is the need of the person with dementia for activity. A pleasurable or absorbing activity can greatly lessen behavioural disturbance. While activities as varied as cooking, art and crafts, and music can be done easily in an institutional setting it is important not to underestimate just how difficult it can be for a carer to instigate.

Case study

On accompanying her husband to a day-unit a small and frail spouse-carer was noted to have bruised arms. On assessment it became apparent that in her anxiety to dress him in time for the unit transport a tussle took place every morning. She would try to get him dressed and he would either respond slowly or resist her efforts. She tried to hurry him along at which point he would grip her arms and on more than one occasion hit her. It seemed he would be cooperative for the first few items of clothing but would grow irritated or distressed by her attentions and it was at this point that resistance and subsequent aggression would start. The intervention to this aggressive behavioural disturbance by the day-centre staff was threefold. First, they reassured her that if he was not ready when the transport arrived

they would wait and help get him dressed. Second, it was suggested she try to get him dressed in stages – walking away if he became resistant at any stage and leaving him for a few moments. Third, a member of the unit came to the house and went through his clothes with his wife and together they selected clothes for everyday use that were easy to put on and put aside shirts with many buttons and trousers needing braces. Ties were dispensed with altogether.

Changing the environment

People with dementia are often highly responsive to the environment they find themselves in. In general terms, the environment should be safe and familiar and unnecessary changes should be resisted. Safety is particularly important to allow a carer to leave a disturbed patient for a little while without worrying. An occupational-therapy assessment of a home environment can be particularly useful to identify potential dangers and to instigate specific measures, such as locking away dangerous tools or kitchen implements. Wandering can be made safe by restricting a person to a specific area but this entails the constant attention to balancing personal autonomy and managing behaviour.

Pharmacological management

Treatments of specific neuropsychiatric symptoms are discussed in chapter 4. Frequently a pharmacological approach is indicated for behavioural disturbance not associated with other symptoms. The most-used class of drugs is the anti-psychotics (Michel and Kolakowska, 1981; Lantz et al, 1990) but antidepressants, anxiolytics, and other sedating drugs have a place. Increasing attention is being paid to the possible effects of cholinomimetic palliative therapies in moderating behaviour.

Antipsychotic medication

Despite widespread use (Michel and Kolakowska, 1981; Lantz et al, 1990; Devanand et al, 1988), published work on the effects of neuroleptics on behavioural disturbance in AD is not comprehensive. However, some randomised, placebo-controlled, double-blind trials have been done – with very mixed results. Some early studies showed little beneficial effect, although more recent studies do concur that a wide range of behavioural disturbance is improved with neuroleptics including the commonly used typical antipsychotics (Barnes et al, 1982; Petrie et al, 1982). There is little to choose between these two drugs (Tsuang et al, 1971), although the beneficial side-effect profile suggests the newer atypical antipsychotics

such as risperidone or olanzapine may be better, and thioridizine should be avoided altogether. Trials suggest that risperidone can be a useful drug, although not free of adverse effects in the elderly (Frenchman and Prince, 1997; Kopala and Honer, 1997). If medication is helpful, but the behaviour continues when it is stopped, depot administration can be used.

It is difficult to understand quite how antipsychotic drugs are efficacious in behavioural disturbance although they undoubtedly are. It is possible that underlying and undetected hallucinations or delusions are treated and in some cases sedation may have a role. However, low-dose neuroleptics are frequently effective and when well administered can reduce behavioural disturbance a lot without any detectable effect on activity, certainly without overt sedation. Some evidence does suggest that neuroleptics can have a harmful effect on cognition and may even accelerate deterioration (McShane et al, 1997; Holmes et al, 1997) and so should only be administered with care. Because of the potential for further impairing cholinergic function, drugs with minimal anticholinergic action are theoretically preferable.

One study has suggested that quality of life is negatively associated with use of antipsychotic medication, although the effect is as likely to be due to the primary symptoms resulting in neuroleptic administration in the first place (Albert et al, 1996). In all cases, however, antipsychotic medication should be kept under regular review and stopped wherever possible. Over the course of time the symptoms of behavioural disturbance will fluctuate and the need for medication may disappear. Too many patients are left on medication, especially in long-term care, and could be withdrawn from medication without ill-effect (Bridges Parlet et al, 1997).

Benzodiazepines

Benzodiazepines have a limited role in the short-term management of behavioural disturbance. Patients with dementia seem to be particularly vulnerable to the adverse effects of benzodiazepines, which can cause considerable confusion in those with cognitive impairment. In addition to confusion and day-time sedation there is evidence of increased falls in elderly people receiving benzodiazepines. Despite this benzodiazepines can be used to good effect in the short-term control of acutely disturbed behaviour.

Other drugs

Antidepressants should always be considered if agitation or apathy are accompanied by other signs suggestive of a mood disturbance. However, even in the absence of any other indications of depression, one antidepressant in particular – trazodone – can be helpful in reducing behavioural disturbances, perhaps

because of its sedating qualities. One study showed an equivalent efficacy of trazodone and haloperidol (Sultzer et al, 1997). Other drugs used to good effect in some studies include propranolol (Shankle et al, 1995) and mood stabilizers such as carbamazepine (Tariot et al, 1998) and sodium valproate (Mellow et al, 1993).

Cholinomimetics

The treatments currently available for AD – the acetylcholinesterase inhibitors – were developed to correct the cholinergic deficiency accompanying neurodegeneration. However, trials of metrifonate (Kaufer, 1998), rivastigmine, and velnacrine (Antuono, 1995) all showed some beneficial effects on behaviour as well as cognition; this is likely to be a specific and not idiosyncratic effect, because cholinergic modulation would be expected to effect behaviour. In line with the results of these trials is the finding that muscarinic agonists in development for treatment of AD also beneficially effect behaviour (Bymaster et al, 1997; Bodick et al, 1997).

Summary

- Behavioural disturbance and neuropsychiatric symptoms are common in AD but not all symptoms are disturbing – either to the patient or the carer.

- Decisions as to whether to treat the symptom should be made according to the level of distress the symptom is causing.
- Good assessment includes a description of the behaviour, its antecedents and consequences. Behaviours have causes and a search for probable cause can be facilitated by remembering that most behaviours are caused by Physical problems, are Intrinsic to the disorder, are related to a specific Activity or are a result of Depression or Delusions (PAID).
- Different causes require different responses.
- Behavioural management can mean changing the behaviour of carer as well as patient.
- Antipsychotics can be efficacious in managing behavioural disturbance – chose medication with little anticholinergic effect.
- Benzodiazepines should be used only with great caution if at all.
- Cholinergic therapies may be efficacious in treating behavioural disturbance.

References

Aarsland D, Cummings JL, Yenner G, Miller, B (1996). Relationship of aggressive behavior to other neuropsychiatric symptoms in patients with Alzheimer's disease. *Am J Psychiatry* **153**, 243–47.

Albert SM, Del Castillo-Castaneda C, Sano M, et al (1996). Quality of life in patients with Alzheimer's disease as reported by patient proxies. *J Am Geriatr Soc* **44**, 1342–47.

Alessi CA (1991). Managing the behavioral problems of dementia in the home. *Clin Geriatr Med* **7**, 787–801.

Antuono PG (1995). Effectiveness and safety of velnacrine for the treatment of Alzheimer's disease: a double-blind, placebo-controlled study (Mentane Study Group). *Arch Intern Med* **155**, 1766–72.

Barnes R, Veith R, Okimoto J, Raskind M, Gumbrecht, G (1982). Efficacy of antipsychotic medications in behaviorally disturbed dementia patients. *Am J Psychiatry* **139**, 1170–74.

Bedard M, Molloy DW, Pedlar D, Lever JA, Stones MJ (1997). Associations between dysfunctional behaviors, gender, and burden in spousal caregivers of cognitively impaired older adults. *Int Psychogeriatr* **9**, 277–90.

Bodick NC, Offen WW, Levey AI, et al (1997). Effects of xanomeline, a selective muscarinic receptor agonist, on cognitive function and behavioral symptoms in Alzheimer disease. *Arch Neurol* **54**, 465–73.

Bridges Parlet S, Knopman D, Steffes S (1997). Withdrawal of neuroleptic medications from institutionalized dementia patients: results of a double-blind, baseline-treatment-controlled pilot study. *J Geriatr Psychiatry Neurol* **10**, 119–26.

Bymaster FP, Whitesitt CA, Shannon HE, et al (1997). Xanomeline: a selective muscarinic agonist for the treatment of Alzheimer's disease. *Drug Dev Res* **40**, 158–70.

Coen RF, Swanwick GR, O'Boyle CA, Coakley, D (1997). Behaviour disturbance and other predictors of carer burden in Alzheimer's disease. *Int J Geriatr Psychiatry* **12**, 331–36.

Cohen CA, Gold DP, Shulman KI, Wortley JT, McDonald G, Wargon M (1993). Factors determining the decision to institutionalize dementing individuals: a prospective study. *Gerontologist* 33, 714–20.

Cohen-Mansfield J (1986). Agitated behaviors in the elderly II: preliminary results in the cognitively deteriorated. *J Am Geriatr Soc* 34, 722–27.

Cooper JK, Mungas D, Weiler PG (1990). Relation of cognitive status and abnormal behaviors in Alzheimer's disease. *J Am Geriatr Soc* 38, 867–70.

Cummings JL (1997). Changes in neuropsychiatric symptoms as outcome measures in clinical trials with cholinergic therapies for Alzheimer disease. *Alzheimer Dis Assoc Disord* 11 (suppl), S1–S9.

Devanand DP, Sackeim HA, Mayeux R (1988). Psychosis, behavioral disturbance, and the use of neuroleptics in dementia. *Compr Psychiatry* 29, 387–401.

Finkel SI, Lyons JS, Anderson RL (1992). Reliability and validity of the Cohen-Mansfield Agitation Inventory in insitutionalized elderly. *Int J Ger Psychiat* 7, 487–90.

Forloni G, Lucca E, Angeretti N, Della Torre P, Salmona M (1997). Amidation of β-amyloid peptide strongly reduced the amyloidogenic activity without alteration of the neurotoxicity. *J Neurochem* 69, 2048–54.

Forstl H, Burns A, Levy R, Cairns N (1994). Neuropathological correlates of psychotic phenomena in confirmed Alzheimer's disease. *Br J Psychiatry* 165, 53–59.

Frenchman IB, Prince T (1997). Clinical experience with risperidone, haloperidol, and thioridazine for dementia-associated behavioral disturbances. *Int Psychogeriatr* 9, 431–35.

Gilley DW, Wilson RS, Beckett LA, Evans DA (1997). Psychotic symptoms and physically aggressive behavior in Alzheimer's disease. *J Am Geriatr Soc* 45, 1074–79.

Gormley N, Rizwan MR, Lovestone S (1998). Clinical predictors of aggressive behaviour in Alzheimer's disease. *Int J Ger Psychiat* 13, 109–15.

Greene JG, Smith R, Gardiner M, Timbury GC (1982). Measuring behavioural disturbance of elderly demented patients in the community and its effects on relatives; a factor analytic study. *Age Ageing* 11, 121–26.

Holmes C, Fortenza O, Powell J, Lovestone S (1997). Do neuroleptic drugs hasten cognitive decline in dementia? Carriers of apolipoprotein E ε 4 allele seem particularly susceptible to their effects. *BMJ* 314, 1411.

Hope RA, Fairburn CG (1992). The Present Behavioural Examination (PBE): the development of an interview to measure current behavioural abnormalities. *Psychol Med* 22, 223–30.

Jost BC, Grossberg GT (1996). The evolution of psychiatric symptoms in Alzheimer's disease: a natural history study. *J Am Geriatr Soc* 44, 1078–81.

Kaufer D (1998). Beyond the cholinergic hypothesis: the effect of metrifonate and other cholinesterase inhibitors on neuropsychiatric symptoms in Alzheimer's disease. *Dementia* 9 (suppl), 8–14.

Kopala LC, Honer WG (1997). The use of risperidone in severely demented patients with persistent vocalizations. *Int J Ger Psychiat* 12, 73–77.

Lantz MS, Louis A, Lowenstein G, Kennedy GJ (1990). A longitudinal study of psychotropic prescriptions in a teaching nursing home. *Am J Psychiatry* 147, 1637–39.

Lukovits TG, McDaniel KD (1992). Behavioral disturbance in severe Alzheimer's disease: a comparison of family member and nursing staff reporting. *J Am Geriatr Soc* 40, 891–95.

Maletta GJ (1988). Management of behavior problems in elderly patients with Alzheimer's disease and other dementias. *Clin Geriatr Med* **4**, 719–47.

Marin DB, Green CR, Schmeidler J, et al (1997). Noncognitive disturbances in Alzheimer's disease: frequency, longitudinal course, and relationship to cognitive symptoms. *J Am Geriatr Soc* **45**, 1331–38.

McShane R, Keene J, Fairburn C, Jacoby R, Hope T (1997). Issues in drug treatment for Alzheimer's disease. *Lancet* **350**, 886–87.

Mellow AM, Solano Lopez C, Davis S (1993). Sodium valproate in the treatment of behavioral disturbance in dementia. *J Geriatr Psychiatry Neurol* **6**, 205–9.

Michel K, Kolakowska T (1981). A survey of prescribing psychotropic drugs in two psychiatric hospitals. *Br J Psychiatry* **138**, 217–21.

Mintzer JE, Brawman Mintzer O (1996). Agitation as a possible expression of generalized anxiety disorder in demented elderly patients: toward a treatment approach. *J Clin Psychiatry* **57** (suppl), 55–63.

Mittelman MS, Ferris SH, Shulman E, Steinberg G (1995). A comprehensive support program: effect on depression in spouse-caregivers of AD patients. *Gerontologist* **35**, 792–802.

Mortimer JA, Ebbitt B, Jun SP, Finch MD (1992). Predictors of cognitive and functional progression in patients with probable Alzheimer's disease. *Neurology* **42**, 1689–96.

Mungas D, Weiler P, Franzi C and Henry R (1989). Assessment of behavior associated with dementia: the Disruptive Behavior Rating scales. *J Geriatr Psychiatry Neurol* **2**, 196–202.

Patel V, Hope RA (1992). A rating scale for aggressive behaviour in the elderly (the RAGE). *Psychol Med* **85**, 211–21.

Petrie WM, Lawson EC, Hollender MH (1982). Violence in geriatric patients. *JAMA* **248**, 443–44.

Pruchno RA, Resch NL (1989). Aberrant behaviors and Alzheimer's disease: mental health effects on spouse caregivers. *J Gerontol* **44**, S177–82.

Quayhagen MP, Quayhagen M (1988). Alzheimer's stress: coping with the caregiving role. *Gerontologist* **28**, 391–96.

Reisberg B, Borenstein J, Salob SP, Ferris SH, Franssen E, Georgotas A (1987). Behavioral symptoms in Alzheimer's disease: phenomenology and treatment. *J Clin Psychiatry* **48**, 9–15.

Russo-Neustadt A, Cotman CW (1997). Adrenergic receptors in Alzheimer's disease brain: selective increases in the cerebella of aggressive patients. *J Neurosci* **17**, 5573–80.

Shankle WR, Nielson KA, Cotman CW (1995). Low-dose propranolol reduces aggression and agitation resembling that associated with orbitofrontal dysfunction in elderly demented patients. *Alzheimer Dis Assoc Disord* **9**, 233–37.

Sultzer DL, Gray KF, Gunay I, Berisford MA, Mahler ME (1997). A double-blind comparison of trazodone and haloperidol for treatment of agitation in patients with dementia. *Am J Ger Psychiat* **5**, 60–69.

Tariot PN, Erb R, Podgorski CA et al (1998). Efficacy and tolerability of carbamazepine for agitation and aggression in dementia. *Am J Psychiatry* **155**, 54–61.

Teri L, Borson S, Kiyak HA, Yamagishi M (1989). Behavioral disturbance, cognitive dysfunction, and functional skill: prevalence and relationship in Alzheimer's disease. *J Am Geriatr Soc* **37**, 109–16.

Teri L, Truax P, Logsdon R, Uomoto J, Zarit S, Vitaliano PP (1992). Assessment of behavioral problems in dementia: the revised memory and behavior problems checklist. *Psychol Aging* 7, 622–31.

Tsuang MM, Lu LM, Stotsky BA, Cole JO (1971). Haloperidol versus thioridazine for hospitalized psychogeriatric patients: double-blind study. *J Am Geriatr Soc* 19, 593–600.

Vernooij Dassen M, Felling A, Persoon J (1997). Predictors of change and continuity in home care for dementia patients. *Int J Geriatr Psychiatry* 12, 671–77.

Wild KV, Kaye JA, Oken BS (1994). Early noncognitive change in Alzheimer's disease and healthy aging. *J Geriatr Psychiatry Neurol* 7, 199–205.

Zarit SH, Todd PA, Zarit JM (1986). Subjective burden of husbands and wives as caregivers: a longitudinal study. *Gerontologist* 26, 260–66.

Sleep disturbance in Alzheimer's disease

3

Although there are those who seem to survive, or even thrive, on little sleep, for most of us sleep is a welcomed and much needed end to the day. Undoubtedly the amount of sleep needed changes with age and the elderly sleep less than the young. However, despite a reduced need for sleep with late age, sleep-pattern disturbances common in dementia are stressful both to patients and their carers and present a common management problem.

Sleep consists of five stages, stage 1 a transitionary phase leading to stage 2, that of light sleep, characterized by phasic changes on EEG. Stages 3 and 4 are periods of deep sleep with EEG slow waves (slow wave sleep [SWS]) whereas stage 5 is that of rapid desynchronised eye movements (REM). In younger adults, stage 2 occupies about half of total sleep time (stages 3 and 4 together 20% and stage 5 or REM sleep 25%). This pattern changes with age and stage 1 sleep periods increase at the expense of stages 3 and 4. In the very elderly stage 5 or REM sleep is also decreased. The causes of the changes in sleep pattern with ageing are not fully known. The amount of sleep needed is almost certainly related to extrinsic factors such as the amount of activity undertaken but also to intrinsic cerebral factors. Many physical illnesses also affect sleep, such as prostatism, chest disease, muscular skeletal pain, and use of alcohol and caffeine. The physical causes of sleep disturbance are all common in the elderly. However, although sleep patterns do change with age, these changes are more frequent and severe in Alzheimer's disease (AD).

Sleep disturbance

Surveys of patients with AD in a hospital setting and in the community have emphasised the degree of disturbance of sleep accompanying dementia. Rates vary from 67% of patients with some sleep disturbance (Cacabelos et al, 1996) to 20% or less (Cooper et al, 1990). One long-term study of nursing-staff observations over 12–18 months found that 24% of nights of AD patients in hospital were disturbed (Bliwise et al, 1995).

Although sleep is disturbed early in the disease process, most of the initial changes are exaggerated responses normally seen in ageing. Most importantly, REM or stage 5 sleep is lost only late in disease progression (Grothe et al, 1998; Vitiello and Prinz, 1989). Early in the course of the disease, activity at night increases and the amplitude of the activity/rest cycle is lower (Satlin et al, 1995). Because activity and wakefulness at night increases, the amount of stage 1 sleep increases at the expense of deep stage 3/4 sleep (Martin et al, 1986; Prinz et al, 1982a; Vitiello and Prinz, 1989). Later in the disease progression REM

sleep is lost and some studies have reported an increased latency period until REM sleep (Montplaisir et al, 1995; Prinz et al, 1982b). Sleep disturbances such as these are not, however, limited to AD; some evidence suggests that the sleep disturbance of vascular dementia can be as severe or indeed worse than that found in AD. Measures of both the amount of REM sleep and REM latency, however, may make it possible to distinguish between depression and dementia (Dykierek et al, 1998; Vitiello et al, 1984).

The pathogenesis of sleep disturbance in AD is not understood, although there is evidence to suggest that cholinergic loss is largely the cause (Montplaisir et al, 1995). Although a complex phenomenon, the control of sleep is to a large extent under cholinergic regulation (Riemann et al, 1994). REM sleep itself is clearly under direct control of cholinergic neurones, in particular the cholinergic tracts running from brainstem nuclei (Everitt and Robbins, 1997) – although cerebral mapping of sleep centres with retrograde transport of tagged markers of the cholinergic system have identified other cholinergic pathways and indeed non-cholinergic influence on REM sleep in the cat (Quattrochi et al, 1998). As cholinergic neurones are lost in AD, this is likely to affect sleep over and above the normal changes of ageing and it is almost certainly the loss of cholinergic projection from the nucleus basalis of Meynert that is responsible for loss of REM sleep in moderate dementia. However, in AD, other evidence suggests a more profound disturbance of circadian rhythms in addition to this loss of regulation of sleep architecture. A sub-group of AD patients appear to have impaired synchronisation of core body temperature and circadian cycles (Satlin et al, 1995). Disturbance of the normal circadian rhythms of the hypothalamic pituitary axis is altered in AD (Martignoni et al, 1990; Suemaru et al, 1991; Wallin et al, 1991).

Circadian-rhythm control, the biological clock, is located in the suprachiasmatic nucleus and lesions within this small structure can cause complete disruption of the normal wake/sleep cycle. In AD loss of circadian rhythms is manifested by increased napping during the day and quite possibly also the phenomenon of sun downing whereby behavioural disturbance is exacerbated in the latter part of the day. The control of circadian rhythm by the suprachiasmatic nucleus (SCN) has been shown, in animal studies, to be closely linked to the external light/dark cycle – a process of synchronisation known as N training. In patients with AD the degree of night-time activity was shown in one study to change according to the season, becoming worse as the days grew longer (Van Someren et al, 1996).

The reason why SCN control of circadian rhythm is altered in AD is unclear but may not be directly due to neuronal loss. Transplantation of transgenic cells overexpressing the amyloid peptide to the SCN of rats caused disruption of circadian rhythm (Tate et al, 1992). Direct evidence of SCN-function abnormalities in AD comes from studies showing altered melatonin rhythms in some, but not all, patients (Uchida et al, 1996).

Sleep disturbance in AD may result from loss of cholinergic influence over REM sleep and altered SCN regulation of circadian rhythms. As may be expected, if there is a direct relation between neuronal loss and sleep disturbance, loss of normal sleep architecture tends to be more severe in those with more severe disease (Bliwise et al, 1995; Ancoli-Israel et al, 1997). The observation that sleep disturbance also correlates with daytime behavioural disturbance (Rebok et al, 1991) may reflect the idea that cholinergic projections to the thalamus regulate sleep disturbance while cholinergic projections to midbrain dopamine neurons are responsible for behavioural disturbance in AD (Everitt and Robbins, 1997). Loss of nucleus basalis Meynert neurons would give rise to both simultaneously. However, in addition to sleep disturbance resulting from the pathogenesis of Alzheimer's disease, changes in sleep may occur commonly in AD because of extrinsic factors. Physical causes of insomnia are common, particularly with increasing frailty, and the decreased activity inherent in moderate AD contributes to increased activity at night.

Sleep disturbance and carers

Loss of sleep itself is distressing for patients and can be of primary concern to carers. However, loss of sleep is almost always accompanied by altered behaviour during wakefulness at night and this has a substantial impact on carers. It has also been shown that even day-time behavioural disturbance is associated with night-time sleeplessness (Rebok et al, 1991). Not surprisingly, sleep disturbance is among the most stressful of behavioural disturbances reported by carers (Donaldson et al, 1998); it is easy to see how loss of sleep in the patient results in loss of sleep in the carer, which will impact on their ability to look after the patient. An escalation can ensue, resulting in a complete loss of morale and breakdown in the home situation.

People with AD vary considerably in their behaviours on waking. Some patients are quiet on waking, although the carer may be aware that they are awake. More commonly, however, the patient on waking, will get up and pace around the home or act as if it is daytime. For this reason the primary focus of treatment of sleep disturbance, at least when the patient lives at home, should be to ensure that the carer gets an adequate night's sleep.

Case history

A 72-year-old man with moderate AD was very well cared for at home by his wife. Other than attending a day centre twice a week, the couple used no other services and indeed no other facilities were deemed necessary. It was a surprise, therefore, when he and his wife were brought by relatives to an emergency admission unit. It appeared that he had begun to wake at night and would get up and attempt to make his wife breakfast. Fearing he would come to some harm, she had taken to sleeping in his bedroom, so she would wake when he did. Not surprisingly, she too began to suffer from severe loss of sleep. When relatives came to visit they found both of them unkempt and distressed. In response a night-time sitter was arranged for one day a week and the carer encouraged to take whatever opportunity she could to catch up on her sleep during the time the patient was at the day centre. Just 3 weeks later she had returned to her former highly competent and organised state and the crisis had passed.

Non-pharmacological intervention

As with all behavioural disturbance, the key to effective intervention is thorough assessment. Assessment of sleep disturbance involves first taking a detailed history of the pattern of sleep – when does the patient sleep by day and by night, whereabouts do they sleep, what do they do before going to sleep, and what happens on waking during the night? A thorough physical assessment is mandatory – is there evidence of respiratory disease, heart failure, peripheral vascular disease, arthritis, chronic back pain, prostatism, or other causes of sleep disturbance? Medication should be reassessed, including attention to over-the-counter preparations such as stimulants or nasal decongestants. The amount of activity by day should be assessed as should the use of alcohol and coffee before bedtime.

Non-pharmacological management of sleep disturbance should always be attempted before drug treatment. The concept of sleep hygiene is useful in managing the sleep disturbance itself. Daytime naps should be prevented wherever possible and activity by day maximised. The relation between daytime activity or mild exercise and increased sleep is preserved in AD. Patients should be encouraged to sleep in a bedroom (not, for example, in a comfortable chair in the living room) and the bedroom should be darkened, peaceful, and used for sleep only. While a small amount of alcohol rarely does harm, excess alcohol use should be prevented. Evening drinks should be warm and milky rather than caffeine-enriched. Attention should be paid to mealtimes; many elderly people in congregate settings are given a substantial and heavy meal at midday and this can induce a soporific state in the afternoon. A light luncheon and a main meal early in the evening (some hours before bedtime) can be helpful for some patients. Evidence exists that sleep patterns can be rectified by interventions such as increased exercise and social contact (Okawa et al, 1991).

A novel non-pharmacological approach that appears promising is the use of bright light to attempt to resynchronise circadian rhythms. From the discussion of the biology of sleep it is apparent that this can only rectify one part of the regulation of sleep but, nonetheless, some evidence has accumulated that, at least for some patients, sleep disturbance is reduced with bright light (Campbell et al, 1988; Satlin et al, 1992; Van Someren et al, 1993; Van Someren et al, 1997).

Pharmacological interventions

There is no effective unproblematical pharmacotherapy for sleep disturbance in AD. Benzodiazepines are, not surprisingly, the most commonly prescribed drugs. However, there is little evidence for effectiveness in AD (McCarten et al, 1995) and much evidence of substantial side-effects, including falls and increased confusion. If benzodiazepines must be used then short-acting compounds are preferable to avoid hangover sedation. However, an ultra short-acting benzodiazepine, triazolam, withdrawn in some countries because of side-effects, had no beneficial effects in AD sleep disturbance (McCarten et al, 1995). Even where effective for increasing sleep, benzodiazepines can only be a very short-term solution for occasional use in crises – to give a carer a short break from sleep disturbance, for example. Longer use will lead to tolerance, with a loss of effectiveness, accompanied by dependence.

Other hypnotics have their place – chloral hydrate is sometimes used but like benzodiazepines can induce severe delirium. Newer hypnotics avoid some of the dependency and tolerance disadvantages of benzodiazepines but have yet to be fully assessed in AD. Sedating antidepressants can be useful, particularly if there is a suggestion that sleeplessness is accompanying altered mood. Trazodone, for example, is highly sedating and can be effective in reducing symptoms of depression and inducing sleep at the same time. Some patients become highly disturbed at night and other pharmacological interventions are necessary as for similar behavioural disturbance by day.

Because increasing cholinergic neurotransmission increases activity and energy, acetylcholinesterases inhibitors would be expected to have an adverse effect on sleep. One of the most commonly reported subjective effects of dementia treatments is that the person seems more 'alive' and 'awake'. Fortunately this does not appear to extend to being awake at night. Trials of acetylcholinesterases inhibitors have shown either no change (Holsboer-Trachsler et al, 1993) or possibly even a small beneficial effect on sleep disturbance (Holsboer-Trachsler et al, 1993; Gillman, 1997).

Managing sleep disturbance: conclusions

Sleep disturbance in AD starts with exaggerations of the sleep loss normal in late life but accelerates to include loss of REM sleep and altered circadian rhythms. As well as neurodegenerative causes of such sleep loss there are many physical causes of sleep loss common in AD patients. Management of sleep disturbance starts with a full and comprehensive assessment. Education and information to carers is sometimes sufficient and always necessary. At times carers worry about decreased sleep in the person they are caring for even if this is causing neither them nor the patient a problem. If the patient loses sleep but does not disturb the carer, then no further treatment may be necessary. If the disturbed behaviour during wakefulness can be managed in some other way, then managing the sleep disturbance itself may not be necessary. However, if the sleep disturbance itself is to be treated, then sleep-hygiene approaches and increasing activity by day are most important and should be attempted first. Pharmacological management alone is rarely effective in the long term.

Sleep disturbance can persist despite aggressive assessment and intervention. In these situations the impact of the disturbance on carers should be minimised. Night-time sitters should be sought and respite periods in residential settings arranged. Although unsatisfactory in many ways, carers can catch up with sleep during the day when the patient attends a day centre. For some patients and their carers, however, persistent and severe sleep disturbance is the main reason for entry into long-term care.

Summary

- Sleep disturbance is an early and common symptom in AD.
- Early in the disease process light (stage 1) sleep displaces deep (stage 3 and 4 sleep); later in the disease process REM (dream) sleep is lost.
- While the cause of sleep loss in AD is not fully understood, increasing evidence points to loss of cholinergic neurons and loss of control of circadian rhythms.
- Sleep disturbance increases day-time and night-time behavioural disturbance and has a profound effect on carers.
- Treatment of sleep disturbance is one of the most productive interventions for patients with AD and their carers – behavioural management being the mainstay of treatment.
- Behavioural management consists predominantly of good sleep hygiene – changing the behaviour so that night and bedrooms are for sleeping whereas day and living rooms and outside are for wakefulness and energy expenditure.
- Pharmacological management is always

problematical and rarely efficacious when used alone.

References

Ancoli-Israel S, Klauber MR, Jones DW, et al (1997). Variations in circadian rhythms of activity, sleep, and light exposure related to dementia in nursing-home patients. *Sleep* **20**, 18–23.

Bliwise DL, Hughes M, McMahon PM, Kutner N (1995). Observed sleep/wakefulness and severity of dementia in an Alzheimer's disease special care unit. *J Gerontol* **50A**, M303–M306.

Cacabelos R, Rodríguez B, Carrera C, et al (1996). APOE-related frequency of cognitive and noncognitive symptoms in dementia. *Methods Find Exp Clin Pharmacol* **18**, 693–706.

Campbell SS, Kripke DF, Gillin JC, Hrubovcak JC (1988). Exposure to light in healthy elderly subjects and Alzheimer's patients. *Physiol Behav* **42**, 141–44.

Cooper JK, Mungas D, Weiler PG (1990). Relation of cognitive status and abnormal behaviors in Alzheimer's disease. *J Am Geriatr Soc* **38**, 867–70.

Donaldson C, Tarrier N, Burns A (1998). Determinants of carer stress in Alzheimer's disease. *Int J Geriatr Psychiatry* **13**, 248–56.

Dykierek P, Stadtmuller G, Schramm P, et al (1998). The value of REM sleep parameters in differentiating Alzheimer's disease from old-age depression and normal aging. *J Psychiatr Res* **32**, 1–9.

Everitt BJ, Robbins TW (1997). Central cholinergic systems and cognition. *Annu Rev Psychol* **48**, 649–84.

Gillman PK (1997). Tacrine for treatment of sleep

disturbance in dementia. *J Am Geriatr Soc* **45**, 1286.

Grothe DR, Piscitelli SC, Dukoff R, Fullerton T, Sunderland T, Molchan SE (1998). Penetration of tacrine into cerebrospinal fluid in patients with Alzheimer's disease. *J Clin Psychopharmacol* **18**, 78–81.

Holsboer-Trachsler E, Hatzinger M, Stohler R, et al (1993). Effects of the novel acetylcholinesterase inhibitor SDZ ENA 713 on sleep in man. *Neuropsychopharmacology* **8**, 87–92.

Martignoni E, Petraglia F, Costa A, Bono G, Genazzani AR, Nappi G (1990). Dementia of the Alzheimer type and hypothalamus-pituitary-adrenocortical axis: changes in cerebrospinal fluid corticotropin releasing factor and plasma cortisol levels. *Acta Neurol Scand* **81**, 452–56.

Martin PR, Loewenstein RJ, Kaye WH, Ebert MH, Weingartner H, Gillin JC (1986). Sleep EEG in Korsakoff's psychosis and Alzheimer's disease. *Neurology* **36**, 411–14.

McCarten JR, Kovera C, Maddox MK, Cleary JP (1995). Triazolam in Alzheimer's disease: pilot study on sleep and memory effects. *Pharmacol Biochem Behav* **52**, 447–52.

Montplaisir J, Petit D, Lorrain D, Gauthier S, Nielsen T (1995). Sleep in Alzheimer's disease: further considerations on the role of brainstem and forebrain cholinergic populations in sleep-wake mechanisms. *Sleep* **18**, 145–48.

Okawa M, Mishima K, Hishikawa Y, Hozumi S, Hori H, Takahashi K (1991). Circadian rhythm disorders in sleep-waking and body temperature in elderly patients with dementia and their treatment. *Sleep* **14**, 478–85.

Prinz PN, Peskind ER, Vitaliano PP, et al (1982a). Changes in the sleep and waking EEGs of nondemented and demented elderly subjects. *J Am Geriatr Soc* **30**, 86–93.

Prinz PN, Vitaliano PP, Vitiello MV, et al (1982b). Sleep, EEG and mental function changes in senile dementia of the Alzheimer's type. *Neurobiol Aging* **3**, 361–70.

Quattrochi J, Datta S, Hobson JA (1998). Cholinergic and non-cholinergic afferents of the caudolateral parabrachial nucleus: a role in the long-term enhancement of rapid eye movement sleep. *Neuroscience* **83**, 1123–36.

Rebok GW, Rovner BW, Folstein MF (1991). Sleep disturbance and Alzheimer's disease: relationship to behavioral problems. *Aging Milano* **3**, 193–96.

Riemann D, Hohagen F, Bahro M, et al (1994). Cholinergic neurotransmission, REM sleep and depression. *J Psychosom Res* **38** (suppl), 15–25.

Satlin A, Volicer L, Ross V, Herz L, Campbell S (1992). Bright light treatment of behavioral and sleep disturbances in patients with Alzheimer's disease. *Am J Psychiatry* **149**, 1028–32.

Satlin A, Volicer L, Stopa EG, Harper D (1995). Circadian locomotor activity and core-body temperature rhythms in Alzheimer's disease. *Neurobiol Aging* **16**, 765–71.

Suemaru S, Hashimoto K, Suemaru K, Maeba Y, Matsushita N, Ota Z (1991). Hyperkinesia, plasma corticotropin releasing hormone and ACTH in senile dementia. *Neuroreport* **2**, 337–40.

Tate B, Aboody Guterman KS, Morris AM, Walcott EC, Majocha RE, Marotta CA (1992). Disruption of circadian regulation by brain grafts that overexpress Alzheimer beta/A4 amyloid. *Proc Natl Acad Sci USA* **89**, 7090–94.

Uchida K, Okamoto N, Ohara K, Morita Y (1996). Daily rhythm of serum melatonin in patients with dementia of the degenerate type. *Brain Res* **717**, 154–59.

Van Someren EJ, Mirmiran M, Swaab DF (1993). Non-pharmacological treatment of sleep and wake disturbances in aging and Alzheimer's disease: chronobiological perspectives. *Behav Brain Res* 57, 235–53.

Van Someren EJW, Hagebeuk EEO, Lijzenga C, et al (1996). Circadian rest-activity rhythm disturbances in Alzheimer's disease. *Biol Psychiatry* 40, 259–70.

Van Someren EJ, Kessler A, Mirmiran M, Swaab DF (1997). Indirect bright light improves circadian rest-activity rhythm disturbances in demented patients. *Biol Psychiatry* 41, 955–63.

Vitiello MV, Bokan JA, Kukull WA, Muniz RL, Smallwood RG, Prinz PN (1984). Rapid eye movement sleep measures of Alzheimer's-type dementia patients and optimally healthy aged individuals. *Biol Psychiatry* 19, 721–34.

Vitiello MV, Prinz PN (1989). Alzheimer's disease. Sleep and sleep/wake patterns. *Clin Geriatr Med* 5, 289–99.

Wallin A, Carlsson A, Ekman R, et al (1991). Hypothalamic monoamines and neuropeptides in dementia. *Eur Neuropsychopharmacol* 1, 165–68.

Psychiatric symptoms

4

Emil Kraepelin, the founding father of European psychiatry, was interested in Alzheimer and his disease not because of an overriding preoccupation with neurological disease but because it appeared that this curious disorder might shed light on dementia praecox or schizophrenia. Kraepelin and Alzheimer recognized that psychotic and other psychiatric symptoms are integral to the phenomenology of this dementia and not epiphenomena. The extent of non-cognitive symptomotology in Alzheimer's disease (AD) and the effects on carers has now come to be more fully realized. Interesting developments have been made in understanding why it is that some patients suffer from psychiatric symptoms, and, most importantly, new interventions for psychiatric symptoms in AD have been developed and old treatments reassessed.

All the major psychiatric syndromes occur as part of AD: depression, anxiety, and psychosis are most frequently encountered but mania, obsessive-compulsive disorders, and even alcohol dependence are also found. However, eliciting psychiatric symptoms in an individual with cognitive impairment is difficult and this has complicated the studies that have tried to find the extent of non-cognitive symptomatology in AD. In this chapter we concentrate on depression and psychosis, noted by Wragg and Jeste (1989) to occur in over a third of patients. The syndromes themselves, while very similar to the same syndromes in the absence of AD, do show some differences and we discuss the presentation, cause, and effects of these two syndromes before dealing with treatment. Although we do suggest some treatment approaches, we note, as have others before us, the lack of data on which to establish evidence-based guidelines. It is disappointing that almost a century after Alzheimer and Auguste that this is the case.

Depression

Prevalence and cause of depression in dementia

Of all the psychiatric syndromes to occur in AD, depression is the most common. However, it has proven difficult to establish just how common depression is, almost certainly because of the obvious difficulty in deciding how to assess altered mood in an individual with cognitive deficits. This problem is not restricted to academic studies. Just as it can be difficult to measure depression in a research setting so too in a clinical setting. Inevitably some depression in patients with dementia will not be recognised and equally some patients will be treated for depression with little effect. There is a

nosological problem too: many of the behavioural manifestations of depression – altered activity and energy level, decreased appetite, altered circadian rhythms – are also manifest in dementia syndromes without any suggestion of changed mood. Nonetheless, despite these difficulties, scales, such as the Cornell Scale for Depression in Dementia, have been developed to help to rate depression in AD (Vida et al, 1994).

Most studies find a high rate of depression in patients with AD, whether they live in the community or hospital. A third or more may have symptoms of depression (Aarsland et al, 1996; Starkstein et al, 1997; Starkstein et al, 1995; Lyketsos et al, 1997; Migliorelli et al, 1995; Burns et al, 1990a) and a fifth may have a major depressive episode (Lyketsos et al, 1997; Burns et al, 1990a; Starkstein et al, 1997; Lyketsos et al, 1997). However, not all studies show such high rates and at least two large studies of community-dwelling patients suggested quite low rates of depression – less than 10% (Brodaty and Luscombe, 1996; Weiner et al, 1994). Just as these studies have challenged the widely held view that depression is common in AD, some have questioned whether there are differences in rates of depression between the dementias. Historically it has always been held that depression is more common in vascular dementia and, indeed, there is some research evidence to substantiate this (Reichman and Coyne, 1995). Other studies of mildly affected individuals (Verhey et al, 1995), however, do not show greater rates of depression in vascular versus AD dementias, and although functional neuroimaging does suggest a greater frontal-lobe loss and concomitant emotional lability in vascular dementia, no increase in depression in these patients was found (Starkstein et al, 1996). It might be that depression in vascular dementia is different to that of AD – more persistent and less clearly related to level of cognitive decline than in AD (Fischer et al, 1990; Ballard et al, 1996).

What are we to make of the confusions in published work? As we have emphasized, the confusion is almost certainly because of the difficulties in diagnosing and assessing depression in those with dementia, a difficulty that is carried over into the clinical field. The weight of evidence, research and clinical, is that depressive symptoms are common in AD, although how frequently this amounts to a full and major depressive episode is uncertain. From the practical perspective depression results in major negative impact upon both the patient and their carer and yet is treatable. It seems appropriate to err on the side of over-diagnosis of depression in AD; the price of over-treatment is small compared with the costs of not treating at all.

The relation between depression and AD is actually even more complex than suggested by the studies cited above. A large body of epidemiological research has suggested that depression may actually be a risk factor for AD – a history of depression being more common in those with AD (Devanand et al, 1996; Jost and Grossberg, 1996; Jorm et al, 1991; Speck et al, 1995). The timing of the depression to the onset of AD is critical; if the depression occurred only a few years before then it could be that the altered mood was a prodromal feature of AD, and not a risk factor for dementia. Some other neurodegenerative conditions such as Huntington's disease have a wide range of psychiatric syndromes that can occur as a prodromal feature (Lovestone et al, 1996). The question whether AD has a depressive prodromal phase is also not resolved as yet. In a study of twins it was shown, for example, that depression increased the risk of AD but that this risk increased the closer the timing of the depression and dementia, suggesting, in this study at least, that most of the apparent increase in risk was due to a prodromal syndrome (Steffens et al, 1997). However, other studies find a preservation of the risk effect even when the depression occurred more than a decade before the dementia (Speck et al, 1995) and it is difficult to envisage a prodrome lasting as long as this.

Why is it that only some people with AD get depressed? The answer to this question may tell us something interesting about either dementia or depression, and so researchers have compared depressed AD patients with non-depressed AD patients according to a variety of measures. Perhaps the most interesting finding was that of Pearlson et al (1990) who found that patients with depression have more relatives affected by depression than did demented but not depressed patients. This suggests a genetic factor may alter the chances of being depressed. This factor has not been found yet; certainly the APOE gene that is associated with AD itself does not seem to be a genetic risk factor for depression in AD (Lyketsos et al, 1997; Cacabelos et al, 1996). It is possible that demented people with depression have a particular loss of neurons that are known to alter mood, such as the serotenergic neurons (Förstl et al, 1992; Chen et al, 1996). Alternatively, clinical experience suggests that some people's personality type is accentuated after becoming demented and that premorbid personality may be a risk factor for becoming depressed after the dementia starts. Some evidence does support this idea but it is difficult to tell whether this is relatives reassessing personality after the patient becomes depressed or whether it is a true association (Strauss et al, 1997). It is commonly thought, and might be expected, that in the early stages some individuals experience lowered mood as a result of their understanding about the disease and their own future. However, our own clinical experience suggests that this is less common than might be expected; we find that patients respond rather well to be told of the diagnosis

and even prognosis and rarely become depressed as a direct result of being told.

Case study

Two elderly brothers had lived together since the death of the wife of the oldest brother; the other brother had never married. For many years they coexisted quite happily, they had been close for much of their lives and had always lived within a few hundred yards of each other. The youngest brother by three years was known to have had AD for more than 2 years and within the past 6 months it became increasingly apparent to the family doctor that the oldest of the two also had memory loss. A referral was made to specialist services. On assessment it became apparent that both brothers had AD, of mild severity in the older and moderate severity in the younger. In addition, both appeared miserable and the carers (a sister who visited often and the children of the older brother) reported that both brothers spent much of the day slumped in chairs facing each other. The younger brother was unable to describe his mood but was losing weight, had no energy, and looked miserable. He often said he wished he was dead. The older brother described feeling miserable and was seen crying frequently. Both brothers slept poorly. A management plan was instigated that included an improved home-care package and regular attendance at a day unit with structured activities. An antidepressant was commenced for both brothers. Six months later the older brother, while not cheerful was no longer as miserable as before. The younger brother continued to look as miserable as previously but was active, sleeping well, and putting on weight.

Assessment of depression in dementia

The case history above shows a few of the problems in diagnosing depression in a person with AD, not least because many of the symptoms of depression also occur in dementia. Inherent biases also make diagnosis difficult; physicians can be slow to recognise depression as part of a dementia syndrome and caregivers can ascribe symptoms of the dementia to depression. Nonetheless, as for behavioural disturbance (Chapter 2), the assessment of depressive symptomatology starts with a careful history from the informant. The symptoms of depression in AD are the same as those in older people without dementia but the most important aspect of assessment is change – has there been a change in mood, has there been a change in activity? The onset of a new symptom suggestive of depression in someone with an established dementia is a very important observation to make. Some of the areas to consider in the assessment of depression in dementia are illustrated in Panel 4.1.

Caregivers can be reliable informants of depression in AD (Victoroff et al, 1997) although repeated studies have shown that caregivers report higher levels of depression than do trained observers. Scales can also be an addition to routine clinical practice; the Cornell Scale for Depression in Dementia (Alexopoulos et al, 1988) is a particularly

Panel 4.1
Assessment of depression in dementia

> **Mood**
> *Does the patient say that they feel depressed or unhappy?*
> *Do they look depressed or cry frequently?*
> *Is there diurnal variation in mood (worse in the morning)?*
> *Does the patient still enjoy the things they used to enjoy (a sing-song; visit of grandchildren)?*
> **Speech**
> *Has speech reduced in rate or volume?*
> *If the patient normally sings or hums do they still do so?*
> **Activity**
> *Has activity declined, does the patient seem to lack energy?*
> *Is the patient overactive; do they wring their hands or act similarly?*
> *Does activity change during the day; is the patient worse in the morning?*
> **Sleep**
> *Has the pattern of sleep changed?*
> *Is there a regular disturbance of night-time sleeping; if so is it early morning waking?*
> **Appetite**
> *Has appetite changed; is there weight loss?*

useful observer-rated scale although it is a measure of depression severity rather than a screening instrument. In clinical practice, however, a combined approach of careful assessment and observation of the patient, an interview with an informant concentrating upon change, together with judicious use of rating scales is the most effective means of detecting depression in AD.

The effects of depression in AD

Quality of life in dementia can be difficult to measure, but all working in the field, both formal and informal carers, agree that good quality of life is not only desirable but achievable. There is no question that depression results in a poor quality of life and experiencing depression during the course of a dementing illness is nothing short of a tragedy. However, apart from the consequences for the patient, it is increasingly clear that depression affects the patient's care needs and also has a major impact upon carers. A depressed patient will function at a level below their ability as a consequence of reduced energy and motivation and require increasing support. Assessments of activity (daily living skills) do show that function is impaired in patients with depression (Lyketsos et al, 1997; Fitz and Teri, 1994) and there is some evidence that depression is one factor leading to aggression (Lyketsos et al, 1999; Victoroff et al, 1998). As discussed in chapter

2, carers find the associated symptoms of AD – the behavioural disturbance and psychiatric problems – far harder to cope with than the disease itself. Carers of depressed AD patients are themselves more depressed and anxious than carers of patients without depression (Donaldson et al, 1998; Brodaty and Luscombe, 1998).

Treating depression in AD

Treating depression in AD is difficult, particularly because the symptoms tend to persist or recur (Levy et al, 1996; Starkstein et al, 1997). When recognised, however, depression should be treated energetically and in many cases, especially in those patients with milder depression, the symptoms can be alleviated or removed entirely. A combination of both pharmacological and psychological therapeutic approaches is necessary, but there is, unfortunately, little evidence from well-conducted studies on which to base a therapeutic programme. This is one of the most important omissions in AD research; while clinical experience can guide us to effective treatments it would be extremely useful to have randomised trial data on which to base guidelines for these most debilitating symptoms.

Various antidepressants have been shown to be moderately effective in treating depressive episodes in AD patients. These trials have included conventional tricyclic antidepressants such as imipramine (Katona et al, 1998; Reifler et al, 1989) as well as the newer selective serotonin reuptake inhibitors (SSRI) and related drugs (Gottfries et al, 1992; Katona et al, 1998; Burke et al, 1997). The choice of antidepressant drug is important because patients with dementia are often frail and may be expected to be more susceptible to side-effects. Falls, possibly due to orthostatic hypotension (a fall in blood pressure on rising) and increased confusion in particular, are a problem with the tricyclic antidepressants. There is another reason to favour the newer SSRI compounds, however. AD is a cholinergic disorder in that the cholinergic neurons are lost first and most in the course of the disorder. The first available antidementia drugs are cholinergic agents. Tricyclic antidepressants have a major anticholinergic effect and would be expected to hasten decline. Neuroleptics also have similar anticholinergic effects and are associated with a more rapid deterioration in cognition (McShane et al, 1997; Holmes et al, 1997). For this reason we would recommend that only drugs without significant anticholinergic activity be used to treat depression in dementia; in practice this means that treatments should only be considered with an SSRI or related antidepressant. Therapy should be started early, as soon as depression is suspected. Given the difficulties of diagnosis that we have discussed above, in practice we would not consider the level of

certainty of depression required in research studies to be a necessary starting point. It is better to have a low threshold for treatment at the expense of treating some patients who may not have a full depressive syndrome than to not treat some depressed dementing patients. Many, perhaps most, patients can be treated in the community but at times it can be helpful to admit a patient to an inpatient facility to ensure compliance and to instigate other therapies. Certainly admission to an inpatient unit as a short-term measure can be successful (Zubenko et al, 1992). The outcome of therapy should be monitored carefully; the report of the carer is probably the most effective means by which to judge the effectiveness of treatment.

Although successful in many cases there is a placebo effect associated with antidepressant therapy, even in those with dementia. Given that the outcome is often assessed partly or in whole through the carer then it may be that the placebo effect is with the carer themselves – they feel something is being done, this reduces their own levels of stress, and this either has an effect on the patient or effects the carer's view of the patient's mood. Other measures may also effect both the patient and their carer – interesting work is being done to examine the interactive style between carers and patients (Fearon et al, 1998; Vitaliano et al, 1993). An increase in pleasurable activities, attendance at a day centre specialising in dementia care, and increased activity itself can all help to alleviate depression in AD. However, there is great scope for developing specific cognitive or behavioural programmes (Teri, 1994).

Mania in AD

Elevated mood is very rare in AD, occuring in less than 4% of patients in the few studies to examine this (Burns et al, 1990a; Lyketsos et al, 1995). However, it does occur, as the following case history shows.

Case study

The husband of a 68-year-old retired occupational therapist (OT) complained to his family doctor that his wife was awake all night and was irritable and aggressive with him. The family doctor visited and then referred the patient to specialist services as a case of hypomania. The patient herself did indeed display many of the features of hypomania. She was very active and found it difficult to sit down. She was dressed in very bright clothes and, according to her husband, this was highly unusual for her. Her make-up was also exaggerated – vivid blue eye-shadow, thickly applied rouge, and a dramatic red lipstick. All were new purchases. She described herself as feeling fantastic but on examination her mood was more irritable than elevated. There were no hallucinatory experiences but she did claim to be head OT of a nearby

hospital, was writing a text book on the subject, and had plans to start an OT school in her flat. These changes in her appearance and character had all occurred within the previous month but in discussion with her husband it became apparent that for at least the past 6 months she had been doing less around the house and her husband and his oldest daughter had gradually taken on most of the shopping, cooking, and cleaning. Neither he nor his daughter had noticed any memory problems and in her current state it proved impossible to do cognitive testing. She was admitted and treated with a combination of lithium and neuroleptics and made a gradual recovery. However, as soon as she was admitted it was apparent that she had difficulty in orientating herself and could never find the bathroom, leading to incontinence on several occasions. As her mood disturbance subsided the extent of her cognitive impairment became clear – she scored 16/30 on Mini Mental State Examination. A discharge home with a comprehensive care package was only temporarily successful and within 4 months of discharge she needed to be placed in a nursing home.

Psychosis and AD

Prevalence and cause of psychosis in dementia

Psychosis, both hallucinations and delusions, are common in AD patients, occuring in 10%–50% of patients (Levy et al, 1996;

Drevets and Rubin, 1989; Burns et al, 1990b). It is difficult to know whether these phenomena have the same quality as those that occur in primary psychotic disorders such as schizophrenia. For example, delusions of theft are very common; whether a person with dementia believing someone has come into the house to steal belongings that have been misplaced is the same category of phenomena as the person with schizophrenia having a complex paranoid delusion is at least open to question. Other delusions also occur and it can be difficult to distinguish between a true delusion and overvalued ideas in someone with cognitive impairments. It is a sad fact that in assessing delusions one must always bear in mind just how vulnerable are the elderly demented. All too often an apparent delusion that belongings have been stolen turns out to have some basis in fact.

Case reports

Mrs A and Mrs B lived within a few hundred yards of each other. Both had AD of moderate severity, having been present for 4 years in the case of Mrs A and more than 6 years in the case of Mrs B. Both were under the care of the same specialist team and received home-care support and regular visits from a community psychiatric nurse. Both complained of visitations to their house. Mrs A believed people were coming through her front door and scampering around her flat. This occurred

at any time of day and night and she kept a wooden stick handy to defend herself. She had never seen these people but believed they stole things from her. As evidence she led her physician into a dark cupboard and showed him a half-empty carton of washing powder. She believed that these intruders were emptying it. Mrs B on the other hand believed her intruders came through an upstairs window. Her belief was that someone came into her house and took her money, or sometimes directly from her bank. On closer questioning of Mrs B it appeared that, in contrast to Mrs A, she did see her intruder and said it was always the same man and sometimes she saw him up a ladder. It turned out that Mrs A was having true delusions but that Mrs B was indeed being visited by her window cleaner who did steal money from her and when seen by Mrs B managed to persuade her to write out cheques for him. The police were informed about Mrs B while Mrs A received pharmacological treatment.

Hallucinations

In addition to delusions of theft and intrusion, frank paranoid delusions also occur but the delusions are rarely systemised or complex. Hallucinations are somewhat less common than delusions but may be striking and complex. Patients may report vague shapes but more frequently will see complex scenes, often of Lilliputian figures or animals.

Auditory hallucinations are less common in the early stages but may occur in the later stages of dementia. It is extremely difficult to assess auditory hallucinations. Carers often report the patient apparently talking to an invisible person but whether this is an hallucination or not is impossible to decide on many occasions. Visual hallucinations are a key symptom of dementia with Lewy bodies, other symptoms of which include fluctuating confusion, signs of Parkinsonism, and falls (McKeith et al, 1996).

Just as for depression the reasons why some people suffer from psychosis as part of AD is not known, although these symptoms are probably associated with the severity of the illness (Drevets and Rubin, 1989) and seem to occur more often in women than in men (Hirono et al, 1998). Some evidence points to genetic vulnerability in some individuals associated with specific loss of some neurons or some regions of the brain. For example, both serotonin-receptor-gene (Holmes et al, 1998) and dopamine-receptor-gene (Sweet et al, 1998) polymorphisms have been associated with psychosis in AD. Loss of certain neuronal populations, in particular those of the dorsal raphe nucleus, has been reported in psychosis in AD (Forstl et al, 1994) and functional neuroimaging studies have suggested that hypoperfusion of the left frontal lobes is associated with delusions whereas parietal lobe hypoperfusion is associated with hallucinatory experiences

(Kotrla et al, 1995). Whatever the cause of psychosis the impact on carers is clearly profound, not least because psychosis is a strong predictor of aggression in patients (Aarsland et al, 1996; Deutsch et al, 1991; Kotrla et al, 1995; Gormley et al, 1998).

Assessment and treatment of psychosis in AD

Assessment of psychosis in clinical practice is entirely dependent upon careful examination, good skills, and sensible use of informant interviews. Scales have been developed (see Chapter 10) for use in clinical research and drug trials including the Neuropsychiatric inventory (NPI) (Cummings, 1997), the Empirical Behavioural Pathology in AD (BEHAVE-AD) rating scale (Auer et al, 1996), and the Manchester and Oxford Universities Scale for Psychopathological Assessment of Dementia or MOUSEPAD (Allen et al, 1996). Occasionally these scales, especially the NPI, find some use in clinical practice to quantify the amount of change after treatment.

Treating psychosis in dementia is important to alleviate suffering in the patient, to improve function (Richards et al, 1993), and to alleviate stress in the carer. However, because psychotic features tend to recur (Levy et al, 1996) and antipsychotic medication carries a high adverse-event rate in the elderly, treatment is difficult. Again, we have little evidence on which to base rational and proven guidelines. One very good randomised placebo-controlled trial did show that the standard dose of haloperidol was more effective than either low-dose haloperidol or placebo (Devanand et al, 1998). For many years there have been calls for more research on the treatment of psychosis in AD (Wragg and Jeste, 1988) and we can only agree that there is a disappointing dearth of evidence. However, neuroleptics clearly do reduce the severity, frequency, and impact of psychosis. The choice of drug is to a large extent based upon side-effect profiles and, as for depression, drugs with anticholinergic effect should be avoided as these can hasten deterioration (McShane et al, 1997; Holmes et al, 1997).

All of the conventional antipsychotic drugs are toxic in the elderly to a greater or lesser extent and because of this some clinicians have begun to use the newer antipsychotics; Clozapine, Risperidone, Olanzapine and others. In younger patients these drugs cause far fewer adverse effects although there is a risk of neutropaenia with Clozapine and this would be even more serious in the elderly. Clozapine was nonetheless used for the treatment of psychosis in AD (Oberholzer et al, 1992) and in dementia with Lewy bodies (Chacko et al, 1993) and appeared to be useful. However, other studies reported a high rate of adverse effects, including increased confusion, falls, and worsening behavioural disturbance (Burke et al, 1998; Pitner et al,

1995). Risperidone may be better tolerated (Herrmann et al, 1998) in the elderly; two large retrospective case-note studies have examined the use of this drug in AD and other dementias. Fewer treatment failures were seen compared with patients treated with conventional neuroleptics, although side-effects did occur in some patients, especially those treated with antidepressant, and other psychotropic drugs were suggested (Zarate CA et al, 1997; Frenchman and Prince, 1997). Nonetheless these studies do suggest that the newer antipsychotics are better tolerated while being at least as efficacious as conventional antipsychotics and should be considered for the treatment of psychosis in AD (Collaborative Working Group on Clinical Trial Evaluation, 1998).

Some exciting evidence is beginning to suggest that specific treatments for AD may also be treatments for psychosis and other neuropsychiatric phenomena. It has been suggested that some of the high incidence of psychosis is due to cholinergic deficit (Cummings and Kaufer, 1996) and it is interesting to note that dementia with Lewy bodies, a disease in which visual hallucinations form an integral part, has if anything more cholinergic deficit than AD (Perry et al, 1990; Perry et al, 1993; Perry et al, 1994). Cholinergic therapies may therefore, theoretically, alleviate non-cognitive symptomatology and some evidence from clinical trials of at least one agent has found an effect on neuropsychiatric syndromes (Kaufer, 1998).

Summary

- The causes of depression and psychosis in AD are largely unknown but some research suggests a subset of patients as being particularly vulnerable because of regional loss of neutrons, loss of particular types of neurons, or genetic factors.
- The impact of depression and psychosis is profound; patients suffer, function declines, and carers are more likely to be depressed and anxious.
- Assessment is a primary medical and specialist task and depends upon a combination of observation of the patient, careful examination of mental state, and interview of informants. Scales may supplement the clinical examination; the Cornell scale for depression in dementia and the NPI appear most useful.
- Treatment should be a combination of: support and information for carers; pharmacotherapy avoiding drugs with anticholinergic effects.
- Consider SSRIs and related drugs as first-line therapy for depression.
- Consider novel antipsychotics and first-line therapy for psychosis.
- Increase social support and create as rich

and rewarding a social environment for the patient as possible.
- Very little evidence is available on the relative merits of different treatment protocols.
- Antidementia drugs may affect the neuropsychiatric phenomena of AD.

References

Aarsland D, Cummings JL, Yenner G, Miller B (1996). Relationship of aggressive behavior to other neuropsychiatric symptoms in patients with Alzheimer's disease. *Am J Psychiatry* **153**, 243–47.

Alexopoulos GS, Abrams RC, Young RC, Shamoian CA (1988). Cornell scale for depression in dementia. *Biol Psychiatry* **23**, 271–84.

Allen NH, Gordon S, Hope T, Burns A (1996). Manchester and Oxford Universities Scale for the Psychopathological Assessment of Dementia (MOUSEPAD). *Br J Psychiatry* **169**, 293–307.

Auer SR, Monteiro IM, Reisberg B (1996). The Empirical Behavioral Pathology in Alzheimer's Disease (E-BEHAVE-AD) rating scale. *Int Psychogeriatr* **8**, 247–66.

Ballard CG, Patel A, Solis M, Lowe K, Wilcock G (1996). A one-year follow-up study of depression in dementia sufferers. *Br J Psychiatry* **168**, 287–91.

Brodaty H, Luscombe G (1996). Depression in persons with dementia. *Int Psychogeriatr* **8**, 609–22.

Brodaty H, Luscombe G (1998). Psychological morbidity in caregivers is associated with depression in patients with dementia. *Alzheimer Dis Assoc Disord* **12**, 62–70.

Burke WJ, Dewan V, Wengel SP, Roccaforte WH, Nadolny GC, Folks DG (1997). The use of selective serotonin reuptake inhibitors for depression and psychosis complicating dementia. *Int J Geriatr Psychiatry* 12, 519–25.

Burke WJ, Pfeiffer RF, McComb RD (1998). Neuroleptic sensitivity to clozapine in dementia with Lewy bodies. *J Neuropsychiatry Clin Neurosci* 10, 227–29.

Burns A, Jacoby R, Levy R (1990a). Psychiatric phenomena in Alzheimer's disease — II: Disorders of perception. *Br J Psychiatry* 157, 76–81.

Burns A, Jacoby R, Levy R (1990b). Psychiatric phenomena in Alzheimer's disease — III: Disorders of mood. *Br J Psychiatry* 157, 81–86.

Cacabelos R, Rodríguez B, Carrera C, et al (1996). APOE-related frequency of cognitive and noncognitive symptoms in dementia. *Methods Find Exp Clin Pharmacol* 18, 693–706.

Chacko RC, Hurley RA, Jankovic J (1993). Clozapine use in diffuse Lewy body disease. *J Neuropsychiatry Clin Neurosci* 5, 206–8.

Chen CPLH, Alder JT, Bowen DM, et al (1996). Presynaptic serotonergic markers in community-acquired cases of Alzheimer's disease: correlations with depression and neuroleptic medication. *J Neurochem* 66, 1592–98.

Collaborative Working Group on Clinical Trial Evaluations (1998). Treatment of special populations with the atypical antipsychotics. *J Clin Psychiatry* 59 (suppl), 46–52.

Cummings, JL (1997). The neuropsychiatric inventory: assessing psychopathology in dementia patients. *Neurology* 48, S10–S16.

Cummings JL, Kaufer D (1996). Neuropsychiatric aspects of Alzheimer's disease: the cholinergic hypothesis revisited. *Neurology* 47, 876–83.

Deutsch LH, Bylsma FW, Rovner BW, Steele C,

Folstein MF (1991). Psychosis and physical aggression in probable Alzheimer's disease. *Am J Psychiatry* 148, 1159–63.

Devanand DP, Marder K, Michaels KS, et al (1998). A randomized, placebo-controlled dose-comparison trial of haloperidol for psychosis and disruptive behaviors in Alzheimer's disease. *Am J Psychiatry* 155, 1512–20.

Devanand DP, Sano M, Tang MX, et al (1996). Depressed mood and the incidence of Alzheimer's disease in the elderly living in the community. *Arch Gen Psychiatry* 53, 175–82.

Donaldson C, Tarrier N, Burns A (1998). Determinants of carer stress in Alzheimer's disease. *Int J Geriatr Psychiatry* 13, 248–56.

Drevets WC, Rubin EH (1989). Psychotic symptoms and the longitudinal course of senile dementia of the Alzheimer type. *Biol Psychiatry* 25, 39–48.

Fearon M, Donaldson C, Burns A, Tarrier N (1998). Intimacy as a determinant of expressed emotion in carers of people with Alzheimer's disease. *Psychol Med* 28, 1085–90.

Fischer P, Simanyi M, Danielczyk W (1990). Depression in dementia of the Alzheimer type and in multi-infarct dementia. *Am J Psychiatry* 147, 1484–87.

Fitz AG, Teri L (1994). Depression, cognition, and functional ability in patients with Alzheimer's disease. *J Am Geriatr Soc* 42, 186–91.

Forstl H, Burns A, Levy R, Cairns N (1994). Neuropathological correlates of psychotic phenomena in confirmed Alzheimer's disease. *Br J Psychiatry* 165, 53–59.

Förstl H, Burns A, Luthert P, Cairns N, Lantos P, Levy R (1992). Clinical and neuropathological correlates of depression in Alzheimer's disease. *Psychol Med* 22, 877–84.

Frenchman IB, Prince T (1997). Clinical experience with risperidone, haloperidol, and thioridazine for dementia-associated behavioral disturbances. *Int Psychogeriatr* **9**, 431–35.

Gormley N, Rizwan MR, Lovestone S (1998). Clinical predictors of aggressive behaviour in Alzheimer's disease. *Int J Ger Psychiat* **13**, 109–15.

Gottfries CG, Karlsson I, Nyth AL (1992). Treatment of depression in elderly patients with and without dementia disorders. *Int Clin Psychopharmacol* **6** (suppl), 55–64.

Herrmann N, Rivard MF, Flynn M, Ward C, Rabheru K, Campbell, B (1998). Risperidone for the treatment of behavioral disturbances in dementia: a case series. *J Neuropsychiatry Clin Neurosci* **10**, 220–23.

Hirono N, Mori E, Yasuda M, et al (1998). Factors associated with psychotic symptoms in Alzheimer's disease. *J Neurol Neurosurg Psychiatry* **64**, 648–52.

Holmes C, Arranz MJ, Powell JF, Collier DA, Lovestone S (1998). 5-HT$_{2A}$ and 5-HT$_{2C}$ receptor polymorphisms and psychopathology in late onset Alzheimer's disease. *Hum Mol Genet* **7**, 1507–9.

Holmes C, Fortenza O, Powell J, Lovestone S (1997). Do neuroleptic drugs hasten cognitive decline in dementia? Carriers of apolipoprotein E ϵ 4 allele seem particularly susceptible to their effects. *BMJ* **314**, 1411.

Jorm AF, van Duijn CM, Chandra V, et al (1991). Psychiatric history and related exposures as risk factors for Alzheimer's disease: a collaborative re-analysis of case-control studies (EURODEM Risk Factors Research Group). *Int J Epidemiol* **20** (suppl), S43–S47.

Jost BC, Grossberg GT (1996). The evolution of psychiatric symptoms in Alzheimer's disease: a natural history study. *J Am Geriatr Soc* **44**, 1078–81.

Katona CL, Hunter BN, Bray J (1998). A double-blind comparison of the efficacy and safety of paroxetine and imipramine in the treatment of depression with dementia. *Int J Geriatr Psychiatry* **13**, 100–8.

Kaufer D (1998). Beyond the cholinergic hypothesis: the effect of metrifonate and other cholinesterase inhibitors on neuropsychiatric symptoms in Alzheimer's disease. *Dementia* **9** (suppl), 8–14.

Kotrla KJ, Chacko RC, Harper RG, Doody R (1995). Clinical variables associated with psychosis in Alzheimer's disease. *Am J Psychiatry* **152**, 1377–79.

Kotrla KJ, Chacko RC, Harper RG, Jhingran S, Doody R (1995). SPECT findings on psychosis in Alzheimer's disease. *Am J Psychiatry* **152**, 1470–75.

Levy ML, Cummings JL, Fairbanks LA, Bravi D, Calvani M, Carta A (1996). Longitudinal assessment of symptoms of depression, agitation, and psychosis in 181 patients with Alzheimer's disease. *Am J Psychiatry* **153**, 1438–43.

Lovestone S, Hodgson S, Sham P, Differ AM, Levy R (1996). Familial psychiatric presentation of Huntington's disease. *J Med Genet* **33**, 128–31.

Lyketsos CG, Baker L, Warren A, et al (1997). Depression, delusions, and hallucinations in Alzheimer's disease: no relationship to apolipoprotein E genotype. *J Neuropsychiatry Clin Neurosci* **9**, 64–67.

Lyketsos CG, Corazzini K, Steele C (1995). Mania in Alzheimer's disease. *J Neuropsychiatry Clin Neurosci* **7**, 350–52.

Lyketsos CG, Steele C, Baker L, et al (1997). Major and minor depression in Alzheimer's disease: prevalence and impact. *J Neuropsychiatry Clin Neurosci* **9**, 556–61.

Lyketsos CG, Steele C, Galik E, et al (1999).

Physical aggression in dementia patients and its relationship to depression. *Am J Psychiatry* **156**, 66–71.

McKeith IG, Galasko D, Kosaka K, et al (1996). Consensus guidelines for the clinical and pathologic diagnosis of dementia with Lewy bodies (DLB): report of the consortium on DLB international workshop. *Neurology* **47**, 1113–24.

McShane R, Keene J, Gedling K, Fairburn C, Jacoby R, Hope T (1997). Do neuroleptic drugs hasten cognitive decline in dementia? Prospective study with necropsy follow up. *BMJ* **314**, 266–70.

Migliorelli R, Tesón A, Sabe L, Petracchi M, Leiguarda R, Starkstein SE (1995). Prevalence and correlates of dysthymia and major depression among patients with Alzheimer's disease. *Am J Psychiatry* **152**, 37–44.

Oberholzer AF, Hendriksen C, Monsch AU, Heierli B, Stahelin HB (1992). Safety and effectiveness of low-dose clozapine in psychogeriatric patients: a preliminary study. *Int Psychogeriatr* **4**, 187–95.

Pearlson GD, Ross CA, Lohr WD, Rovner BW, Chase GA, Folstein MF (1990). Association between family history of affective disorder and the depressive syndrome of Alzheimer's disease. *Am J Psychiatry* **147**, 452–56.

Perry EK, Haroutunian V, Davis KL, et al (1994). Neocortical cholinergic activities differentiate Lewy body dementia from classical Alzheimer's disease. *Neuroreport* **5**, 747–49.

Perry EK, Irving D, Kerwin JM, et al (1993). Cholinergic transmitter and neurotrophic activities in Lewy body dementia: similarity to Parkinson's and distinction from Alzheimer disease. *Alzheimer Dis Assoc Disord* **7**, 69–79.

Perry EK, Marshall E, Perry RH, et al (1990). Cholinergic and dopaminergic activities in senile dementia of Lewy body type. *Alzheimer Dis Assoc Disord* **4**, 87–95.

Pitner JK, Mintzer JE, Pennypacker LC, Jackson CW (1995). Efficacy and adverse effects of clozapine in four elderly psychotic patients. *J Clin Psychiatry* **56**, 180–85.

Reichman WE, Coyne AC (1995). Depressive symptoms in Alzheimer's disease and multi-infarct dementia. *J Geriatr Psychiatry Neurol* **8**, 96–99.

Reifler BV, Teri L, Raskind M, et al (1989). Double-blind trial of imipramine in Alzheimer's disease patients with and without depression. *Am J Psychiatry* **146**, 45–49.

Richards M, Folstein M, Albert M, et al (1993). Multicenter study of predictors of disease course in Alzheimer disease (the 'predictors study') – II: Neurological, psychiatric, and demographic influences on baseline measures of disease severity. (Published erratum in *Alzheimer Dis Assoc Disord* 1993, 7: 239.) *Alzheimer Dis Assoc Disord* **7**, 22–32.

Speck CE, Kukull WA, Brenner DE, et al (1995). History of depression as a risk factor for Alzheimer's disease. *Epidemiology* **6**, 366–69.

Starkstein SE, Chemerinski E, Sabe L, et al (1997). Prospective longitudinal study of depression and anosognosia in Alzheimer's disease. *Br J Psychiatry* **171**, 47–52.

Starkstein SE, Migliorelli R, Tesón A, et al (1995). Prevalence and clinical correlates of pathological affective display in Alzheimer's disease. *J Neurol Neurosurg Psychiatry* **59**, 55–60.

Starkstein SE, Sabe L, Vázquez S, et al (1996). Neuropsychological, psychiatric, and cerebral blood flow findings in vascular dementia and Alzheimer's disease. *Stroke* **27**, 408–14.

Steffens DC, Plassman BL, Helms MJ, Welsh-Bohmer KA, Saunders AM, Breitner JCS

(1997). A twin study of late-onset depression and apolipoprotein E ε 4 as risk factors for Alzheimer's disease. *Biol Psychiatry* 41, 851–56.

Strauss ME, Lee MM, DiFilippo JM (1997). Premorbid personality and behavioral symptoms in Alzheimer disease – Some cautions. *Arch Neurol* 54, 257–59.

Sweet RA, Nimgaonkar VL, Kamboh MI, Lopez OL, Zhang F, DeKosky ST (1998). Dopamine receptor genetic variation, psychosis, and aggression in Alzheimer disease. *Arch Neurol* 55, 1335–40.

Teri L (1994). Behavioral treatment of depression in patients with dementia. *Alzheimer Dis Assoc Disord* 8 (suppl), 66–74.

Verhey FR, Ponds RW, Rozendaal N, Jolles J (1995). Depression, insight, and personality changes in Alzheimer's disease and vascular dementia. *J Geriatr Psychiatry Neurol* 8, 23–27.

Victoroff J, Mack WJ, Nielson KA (1998). Psychiatric complications of dementia: impact on caregivers. *Dementia* 9, 50–55.

Victoroff J, Nielson K, Mungas D (1997). Caregiver and clinician assessment of behavioral disturbances: the California Dementia Behavior Questionnaire. *Int Psychogeriatr* 9, 155–74.

Vida S, Des Rosiers P, Carrier L, Gauthier S (1994). Depression in Alzheimer's disease: receiver operating characteristic analysis of the Cornell Scale for Depression in Dementia and the Hamilton Depression Scale. *J Geriatr Psychiatry Neurol* 7, 159–62.

Vitaliano PP, Young HM, Russo J, Romano J, Magana-Amato A (1993). Does expressed emotion in spouses predict subsequent problems among care recipients with Alzheimer's disease? *J Gerontol* 48, P202–P209.

Weiner MF, Edland SD, Luszczynska H (1994). Prevalence and incidence of major depression in Alzheimer's disease. *Am J Psychiatry* 151, 1006–9.

Wragg RE, Jeste DV (1988). Neuroleptics and alternative treatments: management of behavioral symptoms and psychosis in Alzheimer's disease and related conditions. *Psychiatr Clin North Am* 11, 195–213.

Wragg RE, Jeste DV (1989). Overview of depression and psychosis in Alzheimer's disease. *Am J Psychiatry* 146, 577–87.

Zarate CA, Jr, Baldessarini RJ, Siegel AJ, et al (1997). Risperidone in the elderly: a pharmacoepidemiologic study. *J Clin Psychiatry* 58, 311–17.

Zubenko GS, Rosen J, Sweet RA, Mulsant BH, Rifai AH (1992). Impact of psychiatric hospitalization on behavioral complications of Alzheimer's disease. *Am J Psychiatry* 149, 1484–91.

Biomarkers for diagnosis, prediction and management

5

Huge advances are being made in the understanding of
Alzheimer's disease (AD) and the insights yielded by
molecular biology and genetics may, in the not-too-distant
future, result in specific disease-modifying treatments. There
are, however, other possible clinical implications that result
from a greater understanding of pathogenesis. Most important
of these is the possibility that this work will contribute to
some form of molecular test, which has been something of a
Holy Grail for AD researchers. Elsewhere we discuss the
difficulties of clinical diagnosis and the importance of making
as accurate an assessment of both disease type and severity.
With the advent of specific therapies for AD it is now
incumbent upon clinicians to diagnose AD in the very early
stages, to distinguish between the different causes of
dementia, and to monitor the course of the condition. This
would be much easier if a test were available that would
identify patients early – perhaps even before a dementia was
clinically apparent. A useful test would be one that allowed
the clinician to monitor the progression of the disease
accurately and without bias, or that could distinguish between
AD and other dementias. A test 'for' AD could predict onset
of AD, assess severity of AD, or simply test for the presence of

AD. While no test has been identified yet that fulfils any of these criteria there are some promising developments from the fields of molecular biology and genetics and from neuroimaging (Alzheimer's Association, NIA, 1998; Geldmacher and Whitehouse, 1997; Lovestone, 1999).

Genetic testing and early onset AD

Some forms of early onset dementia are inherited in an autosomal-dominant fashion, although these are relatively uncommon disorders. Mutations in one of three genes appear to be responsible for most of these early-onset autosomal-dominant forms of AD (reviewed in Blacker and Tanzi, 1998; Clarke and Goate, 1993; Cruts and van Broeckhoven, 1998). The amyloid precursor protein (APP) gene on chromosome 21 was the first to be identified but has been shown to be the disease gene in no more than 20 families worldwide. The presenilin-1 gene on chromosome 14 is responsible for more, perhaps most, cases of early-onset familial AD. Presenilin-2 on chromosome 1, on the other hand, is an extremely rare cause of early-onset AD found principally in a culturally distinct group of families now residing in the USA. The determination of the mutations responsible for the disease in these families has been the most important step forward in the understanding of the molecular pathogenesis

of AD and has had real and immediate clinical implications for a few individuals. This advance has become even more pertinent now that mutations have been found in a gene in another dementia that can be difficult to distinguish from AD. A form of frontotemporal degeneration accompanied by symptoms of Parkinson's disease was known to be linked to chromosome 17 in some autosomal-dominant families (Bird et al, 1997; Spillantini et al, 1998). Now it is known that mutations in the tau gene cause this condition and possibly some inherited forms of the very similar Pick's disease as well (Clark et al, 1998; Hutton et al, 1998; Poorkaj et al, 1998). The molecular basis of other secondary dementias, rarely confused with AD, is also known; diseases such as Huntington's disease, dentatorubro-pallidoluysian atrophy (DRPLA) (Koide et al, 1994), and a disorder with migraine, haemorrhage, and dementia, CADASIL (Goate and Morris, 1997).

If a mutation in a family with any one of these disorders is found this confirms the diagnosis; in cases of diagnostic uncertainty it can help to distinguish one dementia from another (Geldmacher and Whitehouse, 1997). Molecular diagnosis has now become a real possibility. For those families with an early-onset clearly familial dementia, the three known familial ADs, DRPLA, HD FTDP-17, and CADASIL can all be diagnosed with absolute certainty in life. The genetic test is only useful as positive identification – failure to find a mutation is meaningful only in those cases where it is known that the pathogenic mutation is present in an affected family member. Also, the test only confirms which dementia is present; it is unable to determine *whether* a dementia is present. Clearly affected individuals possessed the mutation from conception and yet the disorder only starts in adulthood. To detect the disorder in the early stages remains a clinical and at times difficult task. Molecular genetic testing for diagnosis in these autosomal-dominant conditions follows rather than precedes specialist clinical assessment.

Just as in Huntington's disease, finding a mutation responsible for autosomal-dominant AD opens up not only the possibilities of diagnostic testing for affected individuals but also predictive testing for their relatives. Now that specific treatments are available for AD, and because the prognosis of each of the inheritable dementias differs, it is appropriate to search for mutations in all newly diagnosed familial dementias. It is not always straightforward to find the mutations, however, because for the presenilin genes, and to some extent the tau gene, mutations are distributed widely throughout the coding and non-coding sequence of the gene. Nonetheless, departments of medical genetics now have an important role in assisting in the diagnostic process and all such families should be referred to these specialist services.

Molecular diagnostic testing even in these unambiguously familial conditions does carry some ethical and practical consequences for the family. In an autosomal-dominant pedigree all first-degree relatives are at an *a priori* one in two risk. The detection of the mutation in an affected family member does not alter this risk and to that extent no additional information regarding likelihood of suffering from the condition follows for other family members. However, determining a mutation is a different type of knowledge than making a clinical diagnosis. For most families finding a mutation will make concrete the diagnosis and underlie or emphasise the risk that, by virtue of their parentage, they are exposed to. This information can be expected to increase anxiety and in clinical practice does seem to, at least for some family members. Furthermore, finding a mutation in affected family members makes possible predictive testing in other, unaffected, family members and even prenatal testing. These are difficult issues and all families should be involved in the decision to make a molecular genetic diagnosis in their relatives. This step need not involve specialist genetic counselling – not at this stage – but should be seen as the preparatory stage for genetic counselling in the future.

When a disease-causing mutation is detected in an affected family member predictive testing can be offered to unaffected family members. There are important technical problems that have to be considered by a genetics department. For example, if only one family member is affected and available for testing then it can be difficult to establish whether a novel mutation is truly causing the disease or whether it is a non-pathogenic mutation. Another important consideration is penetrance. Although most of the mutations described thus far are fully penetrant – that is, they always cause disease – in at least one family non-penetrance has been reported (Rossor et al, 1996). These considerations and others will be taken into account in advice and information given to family members, but the important point for those clinicians having contact with patients with dementia is that all patients with a clearly familial early-onset dementia should be referred to a specialist genetics department. An algorithm for decision making in relation to genetic testing and dementia is given in figure 5.1

Predictive testing for AD should follow guidelines established for Huntington's disease (Burgess, 1994; Lennox et al, 1994). In brief, testing will be preceded by at least two sessions with two counsellors or geneticists separated by at least 3 months. Some people need more sessions, and follow-up after a test result has been given can be extensive. Such testing should be undertaken only by specialist genetics centres and then with real caution (Scourfield et al, 1997). When conducted in this context predictive testing has been shown to be safer than feared by many in that most people undergoing testing are less anxious and show less psychological distress at follow-up (Bloch et al, 1992; Lawson et al, 1996; Wiggins et al, 1992). However, many individuals choose not to be tested and it may be that a self-selection process operates such that the only people who get tested are those for whom the stress of not-knowing is greater than the stress of possibily receiving bad news.

Molecular genetic diagnostic and subsequent predictive testing should only be embarked upon when a dementia is both clearly early in onset and familial. Where the pedigree is not informative – perhaps because the potential carrier-parent died before the age of onset or there are insufficient family members to determine inheritance – then many genetics departments will offer DNA banking. This can be an invaluable service to subsequent generations. DNA from an affected person can be kept virtually in perpetuity, or at least until relatives decide that they want the DNA to be tested or testing becomes feasible (either because a new gene is discovered or the technology enables more rapid screening for novel mutations). DNA will usually be extracted from a blood sample, although can be obtained by mouth swab and most medical genetics departments will offer DNA banking as a service.

Case study

Two brothers were referred to a specialist

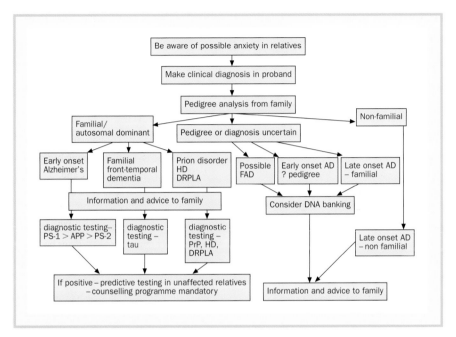

Figure 5.1
Decision making in relation to genetic testing and dementia

clinic for AD genetics by a family doctor. Their family history is shown in Figure 5.2. The mother of the brothers died 5 years previously aged 62 with a dementia that started when she was in her 50s. The dementia was gradual in onset and progression and was accompanied by prominent speech difficulties. Five years after the condition was diagnosed as AD she was almost completely mute. In addition, she was said to have difficulty in walking, frequent falls, and a tremor. Her brother was affected by a similar condition but he was said to be irritable and frequently violent towards his wife. Two years before he too received a diagnosis he had been cautioned by the police for inappropriate sexual behaviour. Very little was known about the maternal grandparent and uncle but it was believed that both lived their last years in a psychiatric institution and both died in their late 50s or early 60s. A cousin is currently being investigated for a change in behaviour.

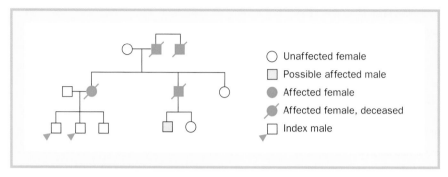

Figure 5.2
Family history of case study

The segregation of the disorder in the family suggests autosomal-dominant inheritance placing the two brothers seeking advice at 50% risk. One of the brothers had pre-teen children and wanted to be able to advise them in due course either that they were at risk of inheriting the condition or that they were not. He felt strongly that when they were of age they should have the opportunity of seeking genetic counselling before contemplating having children. The other brother was newly married and was hoping to have children as soon as possible. However, he felt that if he was going to suffer from the condition he would resolve not to have children because he would not want to subject them to a father becoming demented before they reached adulthood. Both brothers wished at least to consider predictive or presymptomatic testing if this were available.

Predictive testing could not be offered to this family because of uncertainty about the disease gene. This family illustrates some of the problems of retrospective diagnosis. Two family members received a lifetime diagnosis of AD by a consultant psychiatrist. However, some elements of the history of their illnesses must raise the suspicion that in fact the disorder was not AD but a similar disorder. In particular, the early speech difficulties and mutism, the disinhibited behavioural pattern, and the motor disorder all point towards the frontotemporal degeneration complex, some of which is associated with motor-neuron disease and some with Parkinsonism. Given the multiple possible diagnoses then the responsible gene in the family could have been either the APP gene, either of the presenilin genes, the tau gene, or possibly even the Huntington gene. Alternatively, this could have been one of the autosomal-dominant dementias where a gene has not yet been identified. Had material been available from any of the deceased family members then mutation screening at these loci could have been attempted and, following identification of a disease mutation, it would then have been possible to discover whether or not the two brothers carried the same mutation. If they did, then it would be highly likely that they too would develop the condition; if they did not carry the mutation then they could have been reassured that neither they nor their children would succumb to this particular disorder. Some caution would have been expressed if there was any doubt that the mutation was pathogenic (if it were a novel mutation in the same gene, for example) or if penetrance was not known.

As far as the cousin was concerned it would have been appropriate to pursue mutation analysis in the absence of other material from an affected member if he was unequivocally suffering from a dementia. In this situation the test would have been diagnostic and not predictive. However, because she was only under investigation for altered behaviour it was felt inappropriate to conduct diagnostic genetic testing.

These issues are difficult and yet of huge importance to the family. In this family, and in many others, some family members want the information that they do or do not carry a mutation both to settle uncertainty and to make concrete life-planning decisions. Some families and some individuals within all families simply would rather not know. The role of the genetic counsellor is to enable individuals to come to the correct decision for them. Unfortunately this was not possible in this particular family. Had DNA from a blood sample been kept from the mother it might well have been.

Genetics of late-onset AD

For late-onset AD the genetics are more complicated but the issues with respect to counselling more straightforward in that detailed individual genetic counselling is not a prospect for the immediate future. The amount that genetics contributes to personal risk of suffering from AD is not entirely clear. However, genetic factors are the largest single risk factor and the only risk factor, other than age, that is consistently identified in all epidemiological studies (Breitner and Welsh, 1995; Clarke and Goate, 1993; Siooter and van Duijn, 1997). Risk of AD increases dramatically over the age of 75 but for those individuals with a family history this increase in risk is even greater. A series of studies have shown that risk increases to 50% or greater in those with an affected first-degree relative by the age of 90 (Breitner, 1994; Huff et al, 1988; Korten et al, 1993).

It has been estimated that one locus, the apolipoprotein E (APOE) gene, contributes about half of the genetic variance (Owen et al, 1994). There are three common variants of

APOE in the population coded for by three alleles – ε2, ε3 and ε4. Of these, ε3 is the most common and it has been shown that, relative to ε3, the ε4 allele increases risk and the ε2 allele decreases risk (reviewed in Roses, 1996). Perhaps risk, although the term often used, is not quite correct, because it appears that the ε4 allele has the effect of affecting the chances of suffering from AD by lowering the age at which AD occurs (Meyer et al, 1998). Thus, at any given age those carrying e4 alleles are more likely to be suffering from AD than those not doing so. Each individual has two copies of each gene (or two alleles), one inherited from each parent. It follows that the APOE genotype can be either homozygous (two copies) for ε2, ε3, or ε4, or heterozygous as ε2/ε3, ε3/ε4, or ε2/ε4. Those with two copies of e4 are most at risk, at any given age, and those with two copies of ε2 least at risk. However, the APOE gene is not determinative and some individuals with the ε4/ε4 genotype reach old age without dementia and many individuals with no e4 alleles are clearly affected.

APOE has been shown to influence the rate of dementia in many diverse populations and has been unequivocally confirmed as the most important genetic influence on late-onset AD. It is likely that many other genes will also contribute to risk either independently or in interaction with APOE. All of these genes may also influence how individuals respond to environmental risk

factors as diverse as hypertension, head injury, and diet. It has proved difficult to find the other genes associated with late-onset AD. Many genes have been identified by association studies only to fall by the wayside when other studies fail to confirm the findings. A current series of genome studies may, in the long run, prove more reliable at identifying regions of chromosomes that are associated with AD and thus point to the genes that alter risk (Kehoe et al, 1999; Pericak-Vance et al, 1998; Zubenko et al, 1998). What is clear, however, is that the public media has a seemingly insatiable interest in genes and disease and with each new association study there is a flurry of interest. Our experience is that many families are highly attuned to these press reports.

Clinical consequences of late-onset AD genetics research

It has been suggested that a gene that is associated with late-onset AD such as APOE may be of some clinical use for diagnosis, for prediction, or to assist in management (Roses, 1997). Each of these potential uses is of course complicated by the fact that APOE, and almost certainly this will be true for all other genes associated with AD, neither causes the disease nor entirely protects from the disease. Translation of the effect of APOE into risk is consequently problematical. Take diagnosis, for example – some studies have suggested that diagnostic certainty is increased with APOE genotyping (Roses, 1997; Welsh-Bohmer et al, 1997). The diagnosis of AD can be difficult and is complicated by the fact that AD is by far and away the most common form of dementia and neuropathological criteria for AD are present in most of those receiving a primary neuropathological diagnosis of some other condition such as vascular dementia. It follows that any diagnostic process, merely by virtue of mathematics, will be very good at determining when AD is present (tossing a coin would be quite good also) but not so good at determining when another condition is also present and quite bad at determining when AD is absent. Indeed, this is exactly what most studies comparing clinical diagnosis to neuropathological diagnosis show – a high sensitivity and a low specificity. Could APOE genotyping increase the specificity of diagnosis? One very large study examining over 2000 individuals at necropsy (and it is unlikely that a larger study will be completed) has shown that this is the case; combining clinical diagnosis of AD together with APOE genotyping increased specificity of diagnosis at the expense of sensitivity (inevitable as more patients are diagnosed as having some other dementia) for those with an APOE4-positive genotype (Mayeux et al, 1998). However, this was a study conducted in a research setting and whether the same results would be seen in ordinary clinical practice where the range of

complicating medical, psychiatric, and neurological illnesses is greater is difficult to know. Possibly a combination of neuroimaging with genotype analysis may have some role in diagnosis (Small et al, 1996). The conclusion must be that despite much research there is no justification for using genetics in routine diagnostic practice at the present time.

Ultimately the use of APOE genotyping in dementia depends upon how specific the relation is between APOE and AD. As some studies, but not others, have shown an association of APOE with other non-AD dementias such as vascular dementia (Frisoni et al, 1994; Marin et al, 1998) the specificity of the relation between AD and APOE is very much open to question. Until these issues are resolved most groups that have examined the issue think that further data is needed before diagnostic testing using APOE can be recommended in practice.

Predictive testing for AD using the APOE, or any similar gene, is even less likely to find a clinical use than diagnostic testing. Clearly the fact that APOE only alters risk rather than determining disease status precludes predictive testing of the type done for autosomal-dominant conditions such as familial early-onset AD or Huntington's disease. When sufficient prospective community-based studies have run their course it is possible that the degree of risk conferred by APOE or any other gene could be accurately determined. It is possible to envisage a situation where not only could the risk contribution of any one gene be known but also the individual risk of AD based on a combination of genes and environmental factors. Such studies are many years and possibly decades before completion. An early analysis of published studies, however, used an interesting approach that may usefully be replicated when further data from longitudinal population based studies becomes available. By the use of a Bayesian statistical analysis of life time risk at the age of 65 years, it was calculated that the chance of suffering from AD was 15% (Seshadri et al, 1995). Clearly this is considerably higher than the lifetime risk calculated for early in life because by the age of 65 some of life's risks have been successfully lived through. Adding in APOE knowledge changes the risk to 30% if at least one ε4 allele was present and reduced risk to 10% if the individual was free from ε4 alleles. The interest in the study comes from the fact that it is at about the age of 65 that individuals begin to worry about getting AD in the future. Few young people are seriously concerned about what may happen in late old age but as retirement from work and the adjustment to the final period of life (the third age) comes then many begin to wonder what the future holds. We conclude that the change in risk from 15% to either 10% or 30% is too small to be useful. While this is probably true it may be interesting to learn what 65-year-olds themselves think.

Consensus groups in the UK and USA have strongly recommended that predictive or susceptibility testing based upon APOE has no place in genetic counselling for AD (Farrer et al, 1995; Medical and Scientific Committee ADI, 1996; Relkin et al, 1996).

Finally, genetic risk factors for late-onset AD may influence management of patients with dementia. This is most likely to arise through pharmacogenomics – the possibility that genes may influence response to drug therapies (Poirier and Sévigny, 1998). If a particular genotype at a gene or combination of genotypes were to influence response to acetylcholinesterase inhibitors, for example, then this could influence prescribing habits or policies. Some evidence has suggested this may indeed be the case – with those carrying an APOE4 allele being less likely to respond to this class of compounds (Poirier et al, 1995). However, there might be multiple possible explanations for such an observation and in any case other data is contradictory or fails to support these findings. Nonetheless, such drug targeting by genetic make-up may become an important factor for the future.

Genetic testing has little place in the management of dementia of late onset at present. Susceptibility testing is inherently unlikely to ever be possible with a risk-gene as opposed to a determinative-gene, but many clinicians consider even diagnostic testing is premature at the present time. If genetic variation is shown to alter response to drug therapies, this is the most likely door through which genetic testing will ever be of any practical importance in late-onset AD. Whether such developments would be welcomed by patients, their families, or health services remains to be seen.

Molecular biomarkers

Another approach to testing has been to find a molecular biomarker for AD (Alzheimer's Association, NIA, 1998; Hyman, 1998). In some ways this is a more attractive prospect than genetic tasting. Genes are stable, with only a very few curious exceptions you keep what you were born with. To examine a genotype to find whether a disease is present is therefore inherently problematical. Even for autosomal-dominant conditions such as Huntington's disease, determining the presence of the genetic mutation shows only susceptibility and not disease presence – the forgetfulness or depression in an individual carrying the Huntington mutation may be AD or straightforward depression. This is, as we have seen, even more complicated for late-onset AD where the genes are susceptibility genes only. The protein products of genes, on the other hand, change and may therefore provide a marker of the start or perhaps the progression of disease. A series of proteins that might be relevant to AD have been examined in both serum and in cerebrospinal fluid (CSF). While none have at present a proven

clinical use, the results so far have been encouraging to researchers in the area and it is possible that a molecular test will result.

The most promising data so far has come from studies of tau protein in CSF. Tau is a normal microtubule associated protein that is deposited, in a highly phosphorylated state, in the tangles that were recognised as critical to the pathology of the condition by Alzheimer. Some studies have shown that the levels of tau change with disease – increasing as the disease starts but then falling again (Andreasen et al, 1998; Galasko et al, 1997; Riemenschneider et al, 1996). Unfortunately for the prospects of tau as a molecular biomarker test, tau is expressed in neurons only and so can only be accessed in CSF. It seems unlikely that there will ever be such a need for a molecular test that lumbar puncture as a routine clinical test will become a practical possibility. Also the fact that tau levels reflect disease progression non-linearly is an added complication. Other proteins such as products derived from APP, and APOE protein have been measured in CSF and show some correlation, although not as good as for tau, with AD – but have the same handicap of inaccessibility of CSF in a demented person (Lehtimaki et al, 1995; Nakamura et al, 1994; Palmert et al, 1990).

APP, in contrast to tau, is ubiquitously expressed. Products of the APP gene can be measured in serum as well as in CSF and could also reflect the start of the disease (Bush et al, 1992; Martins et al, 1993). Although promising, no single protein has yet been found to be the Holy Grail of a molecular diagnostic test.

Neuroimaging as a biomarker

Of all potential biomarkers, neuroimaging both holds the most promise and is already the most widely used. Structural neuroimaging is a routine in the diagnostic work-up for patients with dementia. Most often CT or MRI is used to exclude other causes of cognitive impairment – tumours and haematomas for example. For a diagnosis of Alzheimer's disease neuroimaging is not required but may be supportive, for vascular dementia it becomes part of the diagnostic process. In research structural neuroimaging has proved invaluable and a number of attempts have been made to quantify and formally assess the atrophic changes seen. In general these methods have little application in diagnosis. However a number of interesting developments take neuroimaging beyond research and beyond simply supporting diagnosis and excluding treatable causes.

Structural imaging – CT and MRI

De Carli et al (1990) reviewed the evidence for the use of Computerised tomography (CT) in diagnosis and found specificity to be more or less independent of the method of analysis but that sensitivity improved with more detailed and quantitative measures. Overall the predictive value of CT is adequate at around 80-85% (Burns et al, 1991; Burns, Jacoby, & Levy, 1991; Jacoby & Levy, 1980; Jacoby, Levy, & Dawson, 1980; Pearlson, Rabins, & Burns, 1991) and this has remained stable as the technology has improved despite increased resolution with modern scanners.

One of the promising developments in neuroimaging was specific imaging of the medial temporal lobe using axial CT scans (20–25° anterior to the normal angle). This angle allows quantification of medial temporal lobe atrophy – one of the earliest sites of AD pathology – and both cross sectional and longitudinal studies were encouraging in finding a more than 90% accuracy rate (Jobst et al, 1992; Jobst et al, 1994; Nagy et al, 1996; Nagy et al, 1999). Unfortunately a recent study suggested that although differentiating dementia from normality the method does not help in differential diagnosis (O'Brien et al, 2000) as a proportion of even normal elderly individuals have hippocampal atrophy (e.g. 30% of all elderly and nearly half of all very elderly in one study (De Leon et al, 1997)). Similarly whilst most studies report that hippocampal atrophy can be used to differentiate AD from vascular dementia (Libon et al, 1998; O'Brien et al, 1997), others found that rates of atrophy of cortical structures are similar in the two conditions (Pantel et al, 1998)

Magnetic resonance imaging (MRI) has a number of distinct advantages over CT – in particular in the improved resolution and the visualisation of soft tissues. Ideal for neuroimaging and MRI is without question the method of choice for imaging white matter pathology. Just as in CT the atrophy of AD is readily detectable by MRIU but less readily differentiated from normal ageing. The medial temporal lobe suffers most, losing between 10 and 50% of volume and MRI visualisation of medial temporal lobe offers even better discrimination from normal ageing than does CT. Even so correct identification of AD patients relative to normals is 88% (O'Brien, 1995), better than the 80–85% of CT but at considerably increased scanning time and expense. These medial lobe changes take place early in the disease process and may therefore be a good biomarker for early change (Bobinski et al, 1999). In line with these findings one important study has assessed whether MRI will help to predict which individuals with mild cognitive impairment are likely to convert to full dementia. In a longitudinal study, a number of MRI measures, in particular atrophy of the entorhinal cortex and the caudal part of the anterior cingulate, were found to differ between individuals who over a 3-year period remained mildly impaired but within the normal range and those who converted to either full dementia or questionable dementia (Killiany et al, 2000).

Discriminant function analyses showed greatest separation between normals and converters (accuracy of 93%) than between questionables and converters (75%). Previous studies also indicated that MRI visualization of the medial temporal lobe might be a useful means both to identify those at high genetic risk of developing dementia and those with mild cognitive impairment of converting to dementia (Convit et al, 1997; De Leon et al, 1997; Fox et al, 1996a; Fox et al, 1996b).

Quantification of atrophy using MRI can be performed using a variety of approaches but one of the most promising is that of serial registration – the comparison of scans, mathematically and visually, taken some time apart. Fox et al have used this approach to show that the rate of brain atrophy in a group with AD was 2.37% (per year, while in normal controls it was 0.41% per year (Fox et al, 2000). Usefully, they translated these figures into power calculations assuming that serial registration was to be used as a biomarker of disease progression. If this is done then based on their figures, then 200 patients would have to be recruited into each arm of a placebo controlled trial to have 90% power to detect a drug effect equivalent to a 20% reduction in the rate of atrophy. Such numbers are achievable and serial registration may prove to be a useful biomarker in such trials.

MRI certainly has a role to play in differential diagnosis but it is no more definitive than CT. Thus no differences were found between DLB and AD (Barber et al, 2000) and even in FTD, where there are clear volumetric differences at post-mortem, MRI differences are seen in some, but not all studies (Frisoni et al, 1996; O'Brien, Desmond, Ames, Schweitzer, Chiu, & Tress, 1997). It is however, the relevance of vascular changes in general and white matter changes in particular that is most problematical. Periventricular lucency and white matter hyperintensities are common in the elderly, and also in depression (Barber et al, 1999; Bracco et al, 1993; O'Brien et al, 1996). These white matter lesions are more common in groups of elderly with dementia but that is not of much help when faced with an individual patient. Their relevance to diagnosis or to measure change remains to be fully established.

membrane metabolism, and *myo*-inositol which significantly affects neuronal survival. MRS has been shown, for example, to detect elevations in myo-inositol occurring before dementia in individuals with AD (Huang et al, 1999) and along with creatinine and NAA to correlate with cognition in late onset AD (Frederick et al, 1997; Lazeyras et al, 1998; Parnetti et al, 1997; Rose et al, 1999; Frederick et al, 1997). Some evidence suggests altered ^{1}H MRS markers in AD and studies of AD populations have reported reductions in NAA which correlated with disease severity, and increases in Choline and *myo*-inositol (Constans et al, 1995; Meyerhoff et al, 1994; Miller et al, 1993; Schuff et al, 1998). Moreover, reduced levels of NAA and increased levels of *myo*-inositol charecterised AD with 83% sensitivity and 98% specificity (Shonk et al, 1995).

Biochemical imaging – Magnetic resonance spectroscopy (MRS)

Magnetic resonance spectroscopy (MRS) is an imaging modality that can be used to measure biochemical change in the living brain, including the neuronal marker N-acetyl aspartate (NAA) (Koller, Zaczek, & Coyle, 1984), creatine, which is involved in phosphate metabolism, choline containing substances (e.g. phosphocholine and glycerophosphocholine) which are crucial to

Functional imaging – SPECT and PET

Single Photon Emission Computerized Tomography (SPECT) can be used to measure blood flow and receptor density amongst other outputs. The method requires injection of a radiotracer although the amount of radiation emitted is low. SPECT has been used to show parietal and temporal pattern of loss in AD (Curran et al, 1993; McKeith et al, 1993; Montaldi et al, 1990; Wyper et al, 1993) but it is really in the differential diagnosis of AD and FTD that SPECT becomes invaluable. Differentiating between the two can be difficult and the SPECT scan is the investigation of choice to dementia the profound frontal blood flow loss that occurs early in the condition (Charpentier et al, 2000; Neary et al, 1990). Future studies using SPECT to image particular functional subsets of neurons will be of interest (Nobuhara et al, 2000; Staley, Malison, & Innis, 1998).

Positron Emission Tomography (PET) is only available in a few centres and is unlikely to have widespread clinical use, even as a bio-marker. However, PET has been used to demonstrate, for example, altered blood flow, altered glucose metabolism and altered receptor density in AD (Blin et al, 1993; Guze et al, 1991; Kumar et al, 1991). These changes may be present very early on indeed and a seminal study showed that those at mild genetic risk of AD had abnormal PET scans decades before the age of onset (Small et al, 1995). Subsequently these data were reproduced using functional MRI – are considerably more accessible technique (Bookheimer et al, 2000).

Summary – neuroimaging

At present structural neuroimaging is essential to exclude certain unusual causes of dementia where these may be suspected following an examination. Structural neuroimaging can be helpful in differential diagnosis although the changes – atrophy and white matter changes

are also common in the elderly. Functional imaging is particularly helpful in differentiating FTD from AD. Promising advances include those that systematically compare serial scans and those that quantify or image the medial temporal lobe. The findings that there are MRI and PET changes decades before the disease do confirm the findings in mild cognitive impairment that imaging may well be useful as a marker of disease change and of prediction of conversion to dementia.

Summary

- Genetic testing for autosomal dominant familial early-onset AD is possible at three genes – APP, preseniline-1 and preseniline-2.
- Genetic testing can be used in these extremely rare families for diagnosis or for prediction.
- Genetic testing for other dementias is also possible – for example at the tau gene in frontotemporal degeneration with Parkinsonism.
- Genetic testing for diagnosis should only be done after discussion with the family – it carries implications for them as all offspring will be a 50% at risk.
- Predictive testing should follow guidelines established for Huntington's disease.
- AD with an onset before the age of 50 years but without a clear-cut pedigree

should be referred to a department of clinical genetics

- Late-onset AD is associated with a risk gene – APOE – and almost certainly other, yet-to-be discovered risk genes.

- Genetic testing in late-onset AD could be used for diagnosis, prediction, or clinical management. The data thus far, however, does not support either predictive testing or pharmacogenomic applications. Consensus groups have not been convinced by the usefulness of APOE testing for diagnosis.

- Although genetic testing in late-onset AD is not recommend relatives may still be concerned about inheriting AD genes and should receive appropriate and accurate information.

- Biomarkers for the presence of disease or for monitoring the progression of the disease are eagerly awaited but not yet available.

- Structural imaging by CT or MRI can be used to aid differential diagnosis.

- Structural imaging of the medial temperal lobe may be useful in predicting conversion to dementia.

- Serial regulation of MRI scans may be useful in monitoring change.

- Functional imaging, especially SPELT, is helpful in diagnosis of frontal lobe demential.

References

Alzheimers Assoc, Natl Inst Aging. Consensus report of the Working Group on: Molecular and Biochemical Markers of Alzheimer's Disease. *Neurobiol Aging.* (1998); **19**, 109–16.

Andreasen N, Vanmechelen E, Van de Voorde A, et al (1998). Cerebrospinal fluid tau protein as a biochemical marker for Alzheimer's disease: a community based follow up study. *J Neurol Neurosurg Psychiatry* **64**, 298–305.

Barber R, Ballard C, McKeith IG, Gholkar A, O'Brien J (2000). MRI volumetric study of dementia with Lewy bodies – A comparison with AD and vascular dementia. *Neurology* **54**, 1304–9.

Barber R, Scheltens F, Gholkar A, et al (1999). White matter lesions on magnetic resonance imaging in dementia with Lewy bodies, Alzheimer's disease, vascular dementia, and normal aging. *J Neurol Neurosurg Psychiatr* **67**, 66–72.

Bird TD, Wijsman EM, Nochlin D, et al (1997). Chromosome 17 and hereditary dementia: Linkage studies in three non-Alzheimer families and kindreds with late-onset FAD. *Neurology* **48**, 949–54.

Blacker D, Tanzi RE (1998). The genetics of Alzheimer disease – Current status and future prospects. *Arch Neurol* **55**, 294–96.

Blin J, Baron JC, Dubois B, et al (1993). Loss of brain 5-HT$_2$ receptors in Alzheimer's disease, *Brain* **116**, 497–510.

Bloch M, Adam S, Wiggins S, Huggins M, Hayden MR (1992). Predictive testing for Huntington disease in Canada: the experience of those receiving an increased risk. *Am J Med Genet* **42**, 499–507.

Bobinski M, De Leon MJ, Convit A, et al (1999). MRI of entorhinal cortex in mild Alzheimer's disease, *Lancet* **353**, 38–40.

Bookheimer SY, Strojwas MH, Cohen MS, et al (2000). Patterns of brain activation in people at risk for Alzheimer's disease. *N Engl J Med* **343**, 450–56.

Bracco L, Campani D, Baratti E, et al (1993). Relation between MRI features and dementia in cerebrovascular disease patients with leukoaraiosis: a longitudinal study. *J Neurol Sci* **120**, 131–36.

Breitner JCS (1994). Genetic Factors. In: Burns A, Levy R, eds. *Dementia.* London: Chapman and Hall, 281–92.

Breitner JCS, Welsh KA (1995). Genes and recent developments in the epidemiology of Alzheimer's disease and related dementia. *Epidemiol Rev* **17**, 39–47.

Burgess MM (1994). Ethical issues in genetic testing for Alzheimer's disease: lessons from Huntington's disease. *Alzheimer Dis Assoc Disord* **8**, 71–78.

Burns A, Jacoby R, Levy R (1991). Computed tomography in Alzheimer's disease: a longitudinal study. *Biol Psychiatry* **29**, 383–90.

Burns A, Jacoby R, Philpot M, Levy R (1991). Computerised tomography in Alzheimer's disease. Methods of scan analysis, comparison with normal controls, and clinical/radiological associations. *Br J Psychiatry* **159**, 609–14.

Bush AI, Whyte S, Thomas LD, et al (1992). An abnormality of plasma amyloid protein precursor in Alzheimer's disease. *Ann Neurol* **32**, 57–65.

Charpentier P, Lavenu I, Defebvre L, et al (2000). Alzheimer's disease and frontotemporal dementia are differentiated by discriminant analysis applied to 99 ^{m}Tc HmPAO SPECT data. *J Neurol Neurosurg Psychiatry* **69**, 661–63.

Clark LN, Poorkaj P, Wszolek Z, et al (1998). Pathogenic implications of mutations in the tau gene in pallidoponto-nigral degeneration and related neurodegenerative disorders linked to chromosome 17. *Proc Natl Acad Sci USA* **95**, 13103–7.

Clark RF, Goate AM (1993). Molecular genetics of Alzheimer's disease. *Arch Neurol* **50**, 1164–72.

Constans JM, Meyerhoff DJ, Gerson J, et al (1995). H-1 MR spectroscopic imaging of white matter signal hyperintensities: Alzheimer disease and ischemic vascular dementia, *Radiology* **197**, 517–23.

Convit A, De Leon MJ, Tarshish C, et al (1997). Specific hippocampal volume reductions in individuals at risk for Alzheimer's disease, *Neurobiol Aging* **18**, 131–38.

Cruts M, Van Broeckhoven C (1998). Molecular genetics of Alzheimer's disease. *Ann Med* **30**, 560–65.

Curran SM, Murray CM, Van Beck M, et al (1993). A single photon emission computerised tomography study of regional brain function in elderly patients with major depression and with Alzheimer-type dementia. *Br J Psychiatry* **163**, 155–65.

De Leon MJ, George AE, Golomb J, et al (1997). Frequency of hippocampal formation atrophy in normal aging and Alzheimer's disease. *Neurobiol Aging* **18**, 1–11.

DeCarli C, Kaye JA, Horwitz B, Rapoport SI (1990). Critical analysis of the use of computer-assisted transverse axial tomography to study human brain in aging and dementia of the Alzheimer type. *Neurology* **40**, 872–83.

Farrer LA, Brin MF, Elsas L, et al (1995). Statement on use of apolipoprotein E testing for Alzheimer disease. *JAMA* **274**, 1627–29.

Fox NC, Cousens S, Scahill R, Harvey RJ, Rosser MN (2000). Using serial registered brain magnetic resonance imaging to measure disease progression in Alzheimer disease: power calculations and estimates of sample size to detect treatment effects. *Arch Neurol* **57**, 339–44.

Fox NC, Warrington EK, Freeborough PA, et al (1996b). Presymptomatic hippocampal atrophy in Alzheimer's disease. A longitudinal MRI study. *Brain* **119**, 2001–7.

Fox NC, Warrington EK, Stevens JM, Rosser MN (1996a). Atrophy of the hippocampal formation in early familial Alzheimer's disease a longitudinal MRI study of at-risk members of a family with an amyloid precursor protein 717$_{VAL-GLY}$ mutation. *Ann NY Acad Sci* **777**, 226–32.

Frederick BD, Satlin A, Yurgelun-Todd DA, Renshaw PF (1997). In vivo proton magnetic resonance spectroscopy of Alzheimer's disease in the parietal and temporal lobes. *Biol Psychiatry* **42**, 147–50.

Frisoni GB, Beltramello A, Weiss C, Geroldi C, Bianchetti A, Trabucchi M (1996). Usefulness of simple measures of temporal lobe atrophy in probable Alzheimer's disease. *Dementia* **7**, 15–22.

Frisoni GB, Calabresi L, Geroldi C, et al (1994). Apolipoprotein E ε4 allele in Alzheimer's disease and vascular dementia. *Dementia* **5**, 240–42.

Galasko D, Clark C, Chang L, et al (1997). Assessment of CSF levels of tan protein in mildly demented patients with Alzheimer's disease. *Neurology* **48**, 632–35.

Geldmacher DS, Whitehouse PJ, Jr (1997). Differential diagnosis of Alzheimer's disease. *Neurology* **48**(Suppl 6), S2–S9.

Goate AM, Morris JC (1997). *Notch3* mutations and the potential for diagnostic testing for CADASIL. *Lancet* **350**, 1490.

Guze BH, Baxter LRJ, Schwartz JM, Szuba MP, Mazziotta JC, Phelps ME (1991). Changes in glucose metabolism in dementia of the Alzheimer type compared with depression: a preliminary report. *Psychiatry Res* **40**, 195–202.

Huang W, Alexander GE, Daly EM, et al (1999). High brain *myo*-inositol levels in the predementia phase of Alzheimer's disease in adults with Down's syndrome: A ^{1}H MRS study. *Am J Psychiatry* **156**, 1879–86.

Huff FJ, Auerbach J, Chakravarti A, Boller F (1988). Risk of dementia in relatives of patients with Alzheimer's disease. *Neurology* **38**, 786–90.

Hutton M, Lendon CL, Rizzu P, et al (1998). Association of missense and 5'-splice-site mutations in tau with the inherited dementia FTDP-17. *Nature* **393**, 702–5.

Hyman BT (1998). Biomarkers in Alzheimer's disease. *Neurobiol Aging* **19**, 159–60.

Jacoby RJ, Levy R (1980). Computed tomography in the elderly. 2. Senile dementia: diagnosis and functional impairment. *Br J Psychiatry* **136**, 256–69.

Jacoby RJ, Levy R, Dawson JM (1980). Computed tomography in the elderly: I. The normal population. *Br J Psychiatry* **136**, 249–55.

Jobst KA, Smith AD, Szatmari M, et al (1994). Rapidly progressing atrophy of medial temporal lobe in Alzheimer's disease. *Lancet* **343**, 829–30.

Jobst KA, Smith AD, Szatmari M, et al (1992). Detection in life of confirmed Alzheimer's disease using a simple measurement of medial temporal lobe atrophy by computed tomography. *Lancet* **340**, 1179–83.

Kehoe P, Wavrant-De Vrieze F, Crook R, et al (1999). A full genome scan for late onset Alzheimer's disease. *Hum Mol Genet* **8**, 237–45.

Killiany RJ, Gomez-Isla T, Moss M, et al (2000). Use of structural magnetic resonance imaging to predict who will get Alzheimer's disease. *Ann Neurol* **47**, 430–39.

Koide R, Ikeuchi T, Onodera O, et al (1994). Unstable expansion of CAG repeat in hereditary dentatorubralpallidoluysian atrophy (DRPLA). *Nature Genet* **6**, 9–13.

Koller KJ, Zaczek R, Coyle JT. (1984). N-acetyl-aspartyl-glutamate: regional levels in rat brain and the effects of brain lesions as determined by a new HPLC method. *Journal of Neurochemistry* **43**, 1136–42.

Korten AE, Jorm AF, Henderson AS, Broe GA, Creasey H, McCusker E (1993). Assessing the risk of Alzheimer's disease in first-degree relatives of Alzheimer's disease cases. *Psychol Med* **23**, 915–23.

Kumar A, Schapiro MB, Grady C, et al (1991). High-resolution PET studies in Alzheimer's disease. *Neuropsychopharmacology* **4**, 35–46.

Lawson K, Wiggins S, Green T, Adam S, Bloch M, Hayden MR (1996). Adverse psychological events occurring in the first year after predictive testing for Huntington's disease. *J Med Genet* **33**, 856–62.

Lazeyras F, Charles HC, Tupler LA, et al (1998). Metabolic brain mapping in Alzheimer's disease using proton magnetic resonance spectroscopy. *Psychiatry Res Neuroimaging* **82**, 95–106.

Lehtimaki T, Pirttila T, Mehta PD, Wisniewski HM, Frey H, Nikkan T (1995). Apolipoprotein E (apoE) polymorphism and its influence on ApoE concentrations in the cerebrospinal fluid in Finnish patients with Alzheimer's disease. *Hum Genet* **95**, 39–42.

Lennox A, Karlinsky H, Meschino W, Buchanan JA, Percy ME, Berg JM (1994). Molecular genetic predictive testing for Alzheimer's disease: deliberations and preliminary recommendations. *Alzheimer Dis Assoc Disord* **8**, 126–47.

Libon DJ, Bogdanoff B, Cloud BS, et al (1998). Declarative and procedural learning, quantitative measures of the hippocampus, and subcortical white alterations in Alzheimer's disease and ischaemic vascular dementia. *J Clin Exp Neuropsychol* **20**, 30–41.

Lovestone S (1999). Early diagnosis and the clinical genetics of Alzheimer's disease. *J Neurol* **246**(2), 69–72

Marin DB, Breuer B, Marin ML, et al (1998). The relationship between apolipoprotein E, dementia, and vascular illness. *Atherosclerosis* **140**, 173–80.

Martins RN, Muir J, Brooks WS, et al (1993). Plasma amyloid precursor protein is decreased in Alzheimer's disease. *Neuroreport* **4**, 757–59.

Mayeux R, Saunders AM, Shea S, et al (1998). Utility of the apolipoprotein E genotype in the diagnosis of Alzheimer's disease. *N Engl J Med* **338**, 506–11.

McKeith IG, Bartholomew PH, Irvine EM, Cook J, Adams R, Simpson A (1993). Single photon emission computerised tomography in elderly patients with Alzheimer's disease and multi-infarct dementia. Regional uptake of technetium-labelled HMPAO related to clinical measurements. *Br J Psychiatry* **163**, 597–603.

Medical and Scientific Committee ADI, Brodaty H, Conneally M, et al (1996). Consensus statement on predictive testing. *Alzheimer Dis Assoc Disord* **9**, 182–87.

Meyer MR, Tschanz JT, Norton MC, et al (1998). *APOE* genotype predicts when – not whether – one is predisposed to develop Alzheimer disease. *Nature Genet* **19**, 321–22.

Meyerhoff DJ, MacKay S, Constans J.-M, et al (1994). Axonal injury and membrane alterations in Alzheimer's disease suggested by in vivo proton magnetic resonance spectroscopic imaging. *Ann Neurol* **36**, 40–7.

Miller BL, Moats RA, Shonk T, Ernst T, Wooley S, Ross BD (1993). Alzheimer disease: Depiction of increased cerebral *myo-* inositol with proton MR spectroscopy. *Radiology* 187, 433–37.

Montaldi D, Brooks DN, McColl JH, et al (1990). Measurements of regional cerebral blood flow and cognitive performance in Alzheimer's disease. *J Neurol Neurosurg Psychiatry* 53, 33–38.

Nagy Z, Hindley NJ, Braak H, et al (1999). Relationship between clinical and radiological diagnostic criteria for Alzheimer's disease and the extent of neuropathology as reflected by 'stages': a prospective study. *Dement Geriatr Cogn Disord* 10, 109–14.

Nagy Z, Jobst KA, Esiri MM, et al (1996). Hippocampal pathology reflects memory deficit and brain imaging measurements in Alzheimer's disease: clinicopathologic correlations using three sets of pathologic diagnostic criteria. *Dementia* 7, 76–81.

Nakamura T, Shoji M, Harigaya, Y et al (1994). Amyloid β protein levels in cerebrospinal fluid are elevated in early-onset Alzheimer's disease. *Ann Neurol* 36, 903–11.

Neary D, Snowden JS, Mann DM, Northen B, Goulding PJ, MacDermott N (1990). Frontal lobe dementia and motor neuron disease. *J Neurol Neurosurg Psychiatry* 53, 23–32.

Nobuhara K, Halldin C, Hall H, et al (2000). Z-IQNP: a potential radioligand for SPECT imaging of muscarinic acetylcholine receptors in Alzheimer's disease. *Psychopharmacology (Berl)* 149, 45–55.

O'Brien J, Desmond P, Ames D, Schweitzer I, Harrigan S, Tress B (1996). Magnetic resonance imaging study of white matter lesions in depression and Alzheimer's disease. *Br J Psychiatry* 168, 477–85.

O'Brien JT (1995). Is hippocampal atrophy on magnetic resonance imaging a marker for Alzheimer's disease? *Int J Geriatr Psychiatry* 10, 431–35.

O'Brien JT, Desmond P, Ames D, Schweitzer I, Chiu E, Tress B (1997). Temporal lobe magnetic resonance Imaging can differentiate Alzheimer's disease from normal ageing, depression, vascular dementia and other causes of cognitive impairment. *Psychol Med* 27, 1267–75.

O'Brien JT, Metcalfe S, Swann A, et al (2000). Medial temporal lobe width on CT scanning in Alzheimer's disease: comparison with vascular dementia, depression and dementia with Lewy bodies. *Dement Geriatr Cogn Disord* 11, 114–18.

Owen M, Liddell M, McGuffin P (1994). Alzheimer's disease. *BMJ* 308, 672–73.

Palmert MR, Usiak M, Mayeux R, Raskind M, Tourtellotte WW, Younkin SG (1990). Soluable derivatives of the beta amyloid protein precursor in cerebrospinal fluid: alterations in normal aging and in Alzheimer's disease. *Neurology* 40, 1028–34.

Pantel J, Schröder J, Essig M, et al (1998). In vivo quantification of brain volumes in subcortical vascular dementia and Alzheimer's disease – An MRI-based study. *Dementia* 9, 309–16.

Parnetti L, Tarducci R, Presciutti O, et al (1997). Proton magnetic resonance spectroscopy can differentiate Alzheimer's disease from normal aging. *Mech Ageing Dev* 97, 9–14.

Pearlson GD, Rabins PV, Burns A (1991). Centrum semiovale white matter CT changes associated with normal ageing, Alzheimer's disease and late life depression with and without reversible dementia. *Psychol Med* 21, 321–28.

Pericak-Vance MA, Bass ML, Yamaoka LH, et al (1990). Complete genomic screen in late-onset familial Alzheimer's disease. *Neurobiol Aging* 19, Suppl S39–S42.

efficacy data based on the MMSE and the Alzheimer Disease Assessment Scale (ADAS-cog, Rosen et al, 1984) has shown that a delay of 6 weeks is required for the maximal cognitive improvement at the highest dose tolerated (Sands et al, 1999). A meta-analysis of twelve randomized clinical trials confirmed a measurable benefit detected by the MMSE and the clinical impression of change, with no influence of age or disease severity on therapeutic response (Qizilbash et al, 1998). An open-label study (Kaufer et al, 1996) and a post-analysis (Raskind et al, 1997) suggest a positive effect on behaviour. Practically speaking, tacrine is not used widely any more, but patients who are doing well on it should not be withdrawn so long as there is evidence of benefit from it.

Donepezil was the second CI widely prescribed worldwide and its use is facilitated by a long half-life allowing daily dosing, good gastrointestinal tolerance with a two-step titration spaced 4–8 weeks apart, and absence of hepatotoxicity. Randomized clinical trials of 6 months duration (Rogers et al, 1998; Burns et al, 1999) have shown that both 5 mg and 10 mg doses daily are effective in improving cognitive and global functioning. The latter study also showed a significant reduction in the rate of loss for instrumental activities of daily living (IADL) at the 10 mg dose. Beneficial effects were reversible after a 6 week wash-out. The long-term follow-up of patients treated with donepezil suggest a

sustained therapeutic benefit with a decline in ADAS-cog and Clinical Dementia Rating (CDR; Morris, 1993) parallel to groups of patients with no specific pharmacotherapy (Rogers and Friedhoff, 1998). Two 1 year trials have shown a sustained improvement for the MMSE above baseline for 9 months (Winblad et al, 1999), and a slowing down of functional decline (Winblad et al, 1999, Mohs et al, 1999). A 6 month trial at more severe stages of AD, operationaly defined as MMSE 5 to 17, showed an improvement in all outcomes, including behaviour and activities of daily living (ADL; Feldman et al, 2000). Practically speaking, donepezil offers the advantage of once-a-day dosing and one-step titration. There is no evidence that certain types of patients are less likely to benefit from donepezil.

Rivastigmine was the third widely available CI worldwide. Randomized clinical trials with the Progressive Deterioration Scale (DeJong et al, 1989) were able to establish stabilization of ADL at doses of 6–12 mg/day (Corey-Bloom et al, 1998; Rösler et al, 1999). Furthermore, there is a clear dose-effect relation for cognition, global impression of change, and ADL. An open-label study in a nursing home setting showed a positive effect on behaviour (Anand et al, 2000). Practically, the use of rivastigmine requires good collaboration between carers and clinicians, to find best tolerated and effective dose for each patient. The recommended monthly titration may facilitate the detection of clinical response by carers and clinicians, often characterized by reinitiation of complex hobbies and IADL. As for donepezil, there is no evidence that certain types of patients are less likely to benefit from this drug. The twice-daily dosing requires more supervision for compliance.

Metrifonate was the CI with the longest duration of action through its active metabolite dichlorvos (Schmidt and Heining, 1998). It could thus be administered once daily, with a good gastrointestinal tolerance. Unfortunately, a reversible proximal weakness of limbs has been noted in some individuals at high doses, leading to its withdrawal for clinical use, despite positive results from trials for cognition (Cyrus et al, 1998), global impression (Morris et al, 1998), ADL (Gélinas et al, 1998) and behaviour (Cummings et al, 1998a). The efficacy of metrifonate does not depend on APOE4 genotype, at least in the short term (Farlow et al, 1998b).

Galantamine is becoming available worldwide as the CI with intrinsic nicotinic activity (Pontecorvo, 1998). Randomized clinical trials have shown efficacy on global impression, cognition, ADL, and behaviour (Raskind et al, 2000; Tariot et al, 2000; Wilcock et al, 2000). Furthermore the follow-up of patients treated for 12 months at 24 mg/day without interruption showed no decline from baseline for cognition using the ADAS-cog, and for ADL with the Disability in Dementia scale (Gélinas et al, 1999). The

therapeutic doses are 16 mg/day and 24 mg/day with twice-daily dosing. It is as yet unclear if the dual CI and nicotinic actions will translate into higher or more sustained symptomatic benefit than other CI in clinical practice (see Chapter 7).

Practical issues in using CIs

This review of published work combined with clinical experience brings out certain common characteristics among CI:

- Gastrointestinal side-effects (nausea, vomiting, diarrhoea, anorexia) are dose-related and transient, avoidable to a great extent by a slower titration up to therapeutic doses (Table 6.2); they may be a limiting factor for their use in patients of small body weight.
- Cardiovascular side-effects (symptomatic bradycardia, syncope) are not frequent, if one is cautious in persons with sick sinus syndrome or other supraventricular conduction defects.
- Less common side-effects are insomnia and exaggeration of depressive symptoms, which can be avoided by ingestion of CI in the morning with donepezil, and treatment of depression before initiating CI therapy.
- The measurable short-term (6 months) improvement in cognition and global functioning is comparable between CI.

Table 6.2
Therapeutic doses of CIs in clinical use

Tacrine (Cognex)	80–120 mg/day	Four times daily
Donepezil (Aricept)	5–10 mg/day	Once daily
Rivastigmine (Exelon)	6–12 mg/day	Twice daily
Galantamine (Reminyl)	16–24 mg/day	Twice daily

- The measurable benefit on ADL has been shown for all CI and is best described as a slowing of decline rather than an actual improvement of specific ADLs.
- The measurable short-term improvement of neuropsychiatric symptoms has been shown with all CI; the pattern is delay in emergence of symptoms, and improvement in apathy. There are variable patterns of impairment for anxiety, depression, hallucinations, which are not likely to be equivalent to atypical neuroleptics (see chapter 4).
- The presence or absence of hepatic P450 metabolism of CI seem to have little importance with drugs commonly used in the management of AD, although vigilance is important to document the possibility of drug interactions at the liver and neuromuscular junction.

As for antidepressants, the choice of one CI versus another will depend on the experience of the clinician, the tolerance and ease of use (especially for patients living alone), and the clinical profile of the individual to be treated (weight, concomitant diseases and drugs). Age and sex do not seem to be determinant factors, nor is the disease stage within the mild-to-moderate range. The clinical relevance of pharmacological characteristics such as selectivity for acetylcholinesterase versus butyrylcholinesterase and reversibility versus pseudo-irreversibility of enzyme inhibition has not been established (Giacobini, 1998).

Responses to CI in clinical practice have been described (Gauthier, 1999) as:

- obvious with return to hobbies and social activities, with or without improvement on MMSE scores; this 'awakening' may last 6–12 months, followed by a slower decline than anticipated for age of onset and severity of dementia at onset on therapy

  Case example. A woman aged 66 has 2 years of progressive decline in recalling recent events and got lost in a familiar camping ground. She is now afraid to go out alone; MMSE 23. Family history of AD (mother and younger sister). After 2 months on donepezil she is described by her spouse as having more drive to do things in the house; MMSE 25. After 6 months she starts to read novels again and wants to participate in volunteer work; MMSE 25. After 13 months she is reading less but keen on word puzzles; MMSE 22.

- modest with a reduction in apathy and increase participation in conversation

  Case example: A man aged 77 has a 2 year history of repeating himself. He stopped hobbies such as woodwork, drawing, oil painting. He needed a navigator to get around with his car. He had no insight into his functional losses; MMSE 24. After 7 months on donepezil he was not driving any more, but was described by his family as being better socially adjusted and having insight into his condition; MMSE 20. Stable after 11 months, MMSE 21.

- absent with clinical decline despite therapeutic doses, or failure to tolerate minimally effective doses

  Case example: A woman aged 80 has 3 years of gradual decline in recall for recent events, and hesitation for the correct word. She stopped driving, knitting, playing cards, and had to move to a residence where meals were provided; MMSE 19. Mood described as sad by her daughters, so sertraline was prescribed. Six months later her mood was described as better, and donepezil

was started at 2.5 mg/day because of concern about low body weight and asthma; MMSE 16. A month later donepezil was stopped because of nausea, diarrhoea, decreased appetite, and weight; MMSE 13.

Since we cannot predict who will improve significantly with a CI, it is recommended to offer a therapeutic trial to every patient in mild-to-moderate stages of AD after the diagnosis has been established, concomitant disorders treated, but realistic expectations should be set to take into account the life experiences of the individual and the stage of illness. This approach uses Goal Attainment Scaling (Rockwood et al, 1996). A semi-structured review of the various symptomatic domains of AD is suggested before initiating therapy to assess the response to treatment that may be symptomatic, e.g. observable improvement above baseline, but also stabilization of symptoms or lesser decline (Table 6.3). The CDR – which systematically explores important domains such as memory, orientation, judgement and problem solving, community affairs, daily activities, hobbies, and personal affairs – may be a useful tool for long-term follow-up of patients on CI, as shown in the open-label long-term follow-up of patients on donepezil (Rogers and Friedhoff, 1998).

If there is no clinically detectable improvement despite the maximum dose recommended or tolerated of a given CI, or if

Table 6.3
Assessment of therapeutic response from cholinesterase inhibitors

---

First 6 months
- *Clinical global impression of change, after interview with patient and carer, taking into account cognition, functional abilities and behaviour.*
- *MMSE or similar objective psychometric test, with patient.*
- *Targeted goals, individualized to patient's past experience and stage of disease.*

Beyond 6 months
- *CDR-like semi-structured interview with patient and carer, looking at memory, orientation, judgement and problem solving, community affairs, daily activities and hobbies, personal care.*
- *Emergence of neuropsychiatric symptoms.*

---

the patient has progressed to a severe stage of AD, the decision to withdraw treatment must be taken after discussion with the patient and carers. In case of rapid deterioration off the drug, it is possible to restart the same or another CI. It is also possible for interested patients and carers to participate in a number of trials with novel symptomatic or stabilization agents (see Chapter 8). Participation in such studies has been shown to be of benefit for patients and families, even on placebo (Albert et al, 1997), is ethically acceptable (Post, 1998), and is required to increase our ability to understand and treat AD more effectively.

Adjunctive therapy to CI

Despite the strength of epidemiological and biological evidence, the safety and therapeutic value of combinations of CI with antioxidants (tocopherol or gingko biloba), oestrogens, and non-steroidal anti-inflammatory drugs remain to be established in randomised clinical trials (Murali Doraiswamy and Steffens, 1998; Pitchumoni and Murali Doraiswamy, 1998). These studies will be helped by the availability of purified extracts of gingko biloba such as the EGb 761 (DeFeudis, 1998), selective oestrogen-receptor modulators (McCormick and Abrass, 1998) and selective cyclo-oxygenase-2 inhibitors (Pasinetti, 1998). It is not recommended at present to routinely add any of these substances to a CI in clinical practice (Patterson et al, 1999). On the other hand, when clinically indicated, antidepressants such as serotonin reuptake inhibitors and atypical neuroleptics such as risperidone, olanzapine, and quetiapine can be combined with a CI. Finally, comprehensive support and counselling programmes have been shown to increase the time spouse-caregivers are able to care for AD patients at home (Mittelman et al, 1996), and a judicious combination of support programmes from community and lay associations to disease-specific pharmacotherapy should prove the best therapeutic approach in the mild-to-moderate stages of dementia.

Summary

- CIs have beneficial effects in trials and clinical practice.
- A range of improvement above baseline can be seen in the first 9 months, best detected by family reports and objective cognitive tests such as ADAS-cog and MMSE.
- After 9–12 months a lesser decline can be observed, best documented by a semi-structured interview for cognitive, functional and behavioural features.
- Autonomic side-effects are common but transient in most people.
- Pharmacotherapy is not a substitute for a well-established diagnosis, education of patient and carer, and supportive programmes.

References

Albert SM, Sano M, Marder K, et al (1997). Participation in clinical trials and long-term outcomes in Alzheimer's disease. *Neurology* 49, 38–43.

Anand R, Koumaras B, Hartman RD, on behalf of Study B452 investigators (2000). The effects of rivastigmine on behavioral symptoms in severe AD patients in a nuring home setting. *Neurobiol Aging* 21 (suppl), S220–21.

Burns A, Rossor M, Hecker J, et al (1999). Donepezil in the treatment of Alzheimer's disease – results from a multinational clinical trial. *Dement Geriat Cogn Disord* 10, 237–44.

Corey-Bloom J, Anand R, Veach J, for the ENA 713 B352 Study Group (1998). A randomized trial evaluating the efficacy and safety of ENA 713 (rivastigmine tartrate), a new acetylcholinesterase inhibitor, in patients with mild to moderately severe Alzheimer's disease. *Int J Geriat Psychopharmacol* 1, 55–65.

Cummings JL, Cyrus PA, Ruzicka BB, Gulanski B (1998a). The efficacy of metrifonate in improving the behavioral disturbances of Alzheimer's disease. *Neurology* 50, A251.

Cummings JL, Vinters HV, Cole GM, Khachaturian ZS (1998b). Alzheimer's disease: etiologies, pathophysiology, cognitive reserve, and treatment opportunities. *Neurology* 51 (suppl), S2–17.

Cyrus PA, Ruzicka BB, Gulanski B (1998). The dose-related improvement by metrifonate of the cognitive performance of Alzheimer's disease patients. *Neurology* 50, A89.

DeFeudis FV (1998). Gingko biloba extract (Egb 761). From chemistry to the clinic. Weisbaden, Germany: Ullstein Medical.

DeJong R, Osterlund O, Roy G (1989). Measurement of quality-of-life changes in patients with Alzheimer's disease. *Clin Ther* 1, 545–54.

Farlow MR, Lahiri DK, Poirier J, Davignon J,

Schneider L, Hui SL (1998a). Treatment outcome of tacrine therapy depends on apolipoprotein genotype and gender of the subjects with Alzheimer's disease. *Neurology* 50, 669–77.

Farlow MR, Lahiri DK, Brashear A, Cyrus PA, Gulanski B (1998b). Metrifonate in the symptomatic treatment of Alzheimer's disease: influence of apolipoprotein E genotype. *Neurology* 50, A88.

Feldman H, Gauthier S, Hecker J, Vellas B, Subbiah P, Whalen E (2000). Benefits of donepezil on global function, behavior, cognition and ADLs in patients with moderate to severe Alzheimer's disease. *Neurology* 54 (suppl), A469.

Folstein MF, Folstein SE, McHugh PR (1975). Mini Mental State: a practical method for grading the cognitive state of patients for the clinician. *J Psychiat Res* 12, 189–98.

Gauthier S (1999). Do we have a treatment for Alzheimer's disease – yes. *Arch Neurol* 56, 738–39.

Gélinas I, Gauthier S, Cyrus PA, Ruzicka BB, Gulanski B (1998). The efficacy of metrifonate in enhancing the ability of Alzheimer's disease patients to perform basic and instrumental activities of daily living. *Neurology* 50, A91.

Gélinas L, Gauthier L, McIntyre M, Gauthier S (1999). Development of a functional measure for persons with Alzheimer's disease: the Disability Assessment of Dementia. *AJOT* 53, 471–81.

Geula C (1998). Abnormalities of neural circuitry in Alzheimer's disease. *Neurology* 51 (suppl), S18–29.

Giacobini E (1988). Cholinesterase inhibitors for Alzheimer's disease therapy: pharmacokinetic and pharmacodynamic considerations. In: Gauthier S, ed. *Pharmacotherapy of Alzheimer's disease*. London: Martin Dunitz, 75–92.

Giacobini E (2000). Cholinesterase inhibitors: from the Calabar bean to Alzheimer therapy. In: Giacobini E, ed. *Cholinesterases and cholinesterase inhibitors*. London: Martin Dunitz, 181–226.

Kaufer DI, Cummings JL, Christine D (1996). Effects of tacrine on behavioral symptoms in Alzheimer's disease: an open label study. *J Geriatr Psychiatry Neurol* 9, 1–6.

Knopman D, Schneider L, Davis K, et al (1996). Long-term tacrine (Cognex) treatment: effects on nursing home placement and mortality. *Neurology* 47, 166–77.

McCormick WC, Abrass IB (1998). Shifting thinking about memory impairment. *Lancet* 352 (suppl), 6.

Mittelman MS, Ferris SH, Shulman E, Steinberg G, Levin B (1996). A family intervention to delay nursing home placement of patients with Alzheimer's disease. *JAMA* 276, 1725–31.

Mohs R, Doody R, Morris J, et al (1999). Donepezil preserves functional status in Alzheimer's disease patients: results from a 1-year prospective placebo-controlled study. Presented at the College of European Neuropsychopharmacology, London.

Morris JC (1993). The Clinical Dementia Rating (CDR): current version and scoring rules. *Neurology* 43, 2412–13.

Morris JC, Cyrus PA, Orazem J, et al (1998). Metrifonate benefits cognitive, behavioral and global function in patients with Alzheimer's disease. *Neurology* 50, 1222–30.

Murali Doraiswamy P, Steffens DC (1998). Combination therapy for early Alzheimer's disease: what are we waiting for? *JAGS* 46, 1322–24.

Pasinetti GM (1998). Cyclooxygenase and inflammation in Alzheimer's disease:

experimental approaches and clinical interventions. *J Neurosci Res* **54**, 1–6.

Patterson C, Gauthier S, Bergman H, et al (1999). The recognition, assessment and management of dementing disorders: conclusions from the Canadian consensus conference on dementia. *Can Med Assoc J* **160** (suppl), S1–20.

Pitchumoni SS, Murali Doraiswamy P (1998). Current status of antioxidant therapy for Alzheimer's disease. *JAGS* **46**, 1566–72.

Poirier J, Delisle MC, Quirion R, et al (1995). Apoloprotein in E4 allele as a predictor of cholinergic deficits and treatment outcomes in Alzheimer's disease. *Proc Natl Acad Sci USA* **92**, 12260–64.

Pontecorvo MJ (1998). Clinical development of galantamine: evaluation of a compound with possible acetylcholinesterase inhibiting and nicotinic modulatory activity. *Neurobiol Aging* **19**, 57.

Post SG (1998). Societal and ethical considerations. In: Gauthier S, ed. *Pharmacotherapy of Alzheimer's disease.* London: Martin Dunitz, 113–22.

Qizilbash N, Whitehead A, Higgins J, et al (1998). Cholinesterase inhibition for Alzheimer disease: a meta-analysis of the tacrine trials. *JAMA* **280**, 1777–82.

Raskind MA, Sadowsky CH, Sigmund WR, Beitler PJ, Auster SB (1997). Effects of tacrine on language, praxis and concognitive behavioral problems in Alzheimer's disease. *Arch Neurol* **54**, 836–40.

Raskind MA, Peskind ER, Wessel T, Yuan W, and the Galantamine USA-1 Study Group (2000). Galantamine in AD: a 6-month randomized, placebo-controlled trial with a 6-month extension. *Neurology* **54**, 2261–68.

Rockwood K, Stoole P, Howard K, Mallery L

(1996). Use of goal attainment scaling to measure treatment effects in an anti-dementia drug trial. *Neuroepidemiology* **15**, 330–38.

Rogers SL, Farlow MR, Doody RS, Mohs R, Friedhoff LT, and the Donepezil Study Group (1998). A 24-week, double-blind, placebo-controlled trial of donepezil in patients with Alzheimer's disease. *Neurology* **50**, 136–45.

Rogers SL, Friedhoff LT (1998). Long-term efficacy and safety of donepezil in the treatment of Alzheimer's disease: an interim analysis of the results of a US multicentre open label extension study. *Europ Neuropsychopharmacol* **8**, 67–75.

Rosen WG, Mohs RC, Davis KL (1984). A new rating scale for Alzheimer's disease. *Am J Psychiatry* **141**, 1356–64.

Rösler M, Anand R, Cicin-Sain A, et al (1999). Efficacy and safety of rivastigmine in patients with Alzheimer's disease: results of an international, 26-week, multicentre, randomised, placebo-controlled trial. *BMJ* **318**, 633–38.

Sands LP, Katz I, Schneider L (1999). Assessing individual, patients for cognitive benefits from acetylcholinesterase inhibitors. *Alzheimer Dis Assoc Dis* **13**, 26–33.

Schmidt BH, Heinig R (1998). The pharmacological basis for metrifonate's favourable tolerability in the treatment of Alzheimer's disease. *Dement Geriatr Cogn Disord* **9** (suppl), 15–19.

Sclan SG, Reisberg B (1992). Functional Assessment Staging (FAST) in Alzheimer's disease: reliability, validity, and ordinality. *Int Psychogeriatr* **4** (suppl), 55–69.

Snowdon DA, Greiner LH, Mortimer JA, Riley KP, Greiner PA, Markesbery WR (1997). Brain infarction and the clinical expression of Alzheimer disease: the Nun Study. *JAMA* **277**, 813–17.

Tariot PN, Solomon PR, Morris JC, et al (2000). A 5-month, randomized, placebo-controlled trial of galantamine in AD. *Neurology* **54**, 2269–76.

Wilcock GK, Lilienfekd S, Gaens E, on behalf of the Galantamine International Study Group (2000). Efficacy and safety of galantamine in patients with mild to moderate Alzheimer's disease: multicentre randomised controlled trial. *BMJ* **321**, 1–7.

Winblad B, Engedal K, Soininen H, et al (1999). Donepezil enhances global function, cognition and activities of daily living compared with placebo in a one year, double-blind trial in patients with mild to moderate Alzheimer's disease. *Int Psychogeriatr* **11** (suppl), 138.

Beyond cholinesterase inhibition

7

The discovery that the cholinergic system is lost first and to the greatest degree in Alzheimer's disease (AD) unleashed a course of research spanning more than two decades that has resulted in efficacious and targeted therapies for AD treatment. The compounds that provided this success were cholinesterase inhibitors but drugs acting upon other transmitter systems may also have value in AD and other means of modulating the cholinergic system may be as important in terms of therapy as cholinesterase inhibitors.

Cholinergic precursors and muscarinic agonists

The various attempts to replace lost cholinergic function in AD provide a textbook example of rational therapeutics and neurotransmitters (Greenwald and Davis, 1983). Essentially, four key strategies have been adopted to try to enhance cholinergic neurotransmission: driving production, increasing release, preventing breakdown, and direct replacement. Attempts to increase production of acetylcholine were among the first treatment strategies in AD. Acetylcholine is generated from phosphatidylcholine, or lecithin, and acetyl-CoA. It was logical therefore to try to drive production of acetylcholine by increasing the amount of bioavailable precursors. Lecithin is a normal dietary factor and available in many health-food outlets as a dietary supplement. Trials of high-dose lecithin (20–25 g/day derived from soya) were done but were found to have hardly any effect on cognition (Little et al, 1985).

Another, apparently unsuccessful but logical approach, was to use direct replacement of acetylcholine by use of postsynaptic agonists. The cholinergic system stimulates both muscarinic and nicotinic receptors, all of which have multiple isoforms and some of which are both presynaptic and postsynaptic. Choosing the target receptor, therefore, was not an easy task. Blockade of muscarinic receptors by scopolamine results in cognitive loss and some muscarinic agonists have been developed as potential therapies in AD. Several of these compounds display preferential activity to the M1 muscarinic receptor, which has the benefit of reducing the possibility of adverse events following peripheral muscarinic agonism. Over a very short period infusion of a muscarinic agonist resulted in some cognitive improvements in patients with AD (Raffaele et al, 1991), offering some preliminary support for this approach. The first data from randomized clinical trials were with Xanomeline – an M1/M4 agonist. The results showed a small but significant improvement in cognitive,

behavioural, and global assessments (Bodick et al, 1997). However, in a subsequent trial xanomeline showed no effects on the Alzheimer Disease Assessment Scale (ADAS-cog) when analysed by the most conservative intention-to-treat analysis (Veroff et al, 1998) although completed analysis and analysis of other cognitive measures did show some positive and significant benefits from the drug. A number of other muscarinic compounds have been produced, including talsaclidine, milameline, and Lu 25-109M. However, these other muscarinic agonists have also failed to live up to expectations with none reporting significant benefits in trials (Thal et al, 2000).

Cholinergic replacement therapy and disease modification

The trials of muscarinic agonists reported thus far are short-term studies concentrating upon symptomatic response. However, it may be that this is the wrong target for the muscarinic receptor agonist because there is some evidence that the most interesting effects of the drugs is to modify disease processes. Amyloid precursor protein (APP) is metabolized in neurons by three proteases termed α-secretase, γ-secretase and β-secretase (or beta-site APP-cleaving enzyme [BACE]) with combined β-secretase and γ-secretase cleavage together resulting in generation of the amyloid peptide that is deposited in plaques in AD. On the other hand, cleavage of the APP molecule by α-secretase divides the amyloid moiety in half and prevents generation of amyloid. An important question remains whether amyloidogenic and non-amyloidogenic metabolism are truly reciprocal in neurons but, nevertheless, the inhibition of β-secretase and γ-secretase and enhancment of α-secretase are important potential disease-modifying therapies. β-Secretase and γ-secretase inhibitors are being actively sought but α-secretase enhancers have already been found. α-Secretase is one of the delightfully named ADAMS (A Disintegrin And Metalloprotease) family of enzymes activated by protein kinase C (PKC). This enzyme is a common second messenger in signalling and is coupled to the M1 and M3 muscarinic receptors. It follows that stimulating these receptors should increase non-amyloidogenic metabolism of APP. This has now been shown with several different muscarinic agonists. Xanomeline, talsaclidine, and Lu 25-109 have all been shown to increase non-amyloidogenic APP metabolism in transfected cells and Lu 25-109 has been shown to do the same in brain slices (Eckols et al, 1995; Muller et al, 1998). In transfected cells mimicking familial AD, xanomeline also has been shown to reduce amyloidogenic metabolism, adding further weight to the suggestion that this may be a useful strategy to modify disease (DeLapp et al, 1998).

As well as favourably altering APP metabolism the muscarinic agonists may have an effect on tau metabolism. In AD neurofibrillary tangles are composed of highly phosphorylated tau and, although it has yet to be proven that tau phosphorylation precedes tangle formation, reduction of tau phosphorylation is an important potential strategy in AD. Possibly the most important target, certainly the most obvious, is glycogen synthase kinase-3 (GSK-3), a neuronal kinase that readily phosphorylates tau. GSK-3 is inhibited by PKC just as α-secretase is activated by PKC. It follows that muscarinic agonists may reduce tau phosphorylation. Just as the parallel prediction for APP metabolism was borne out by experiments on cells so too have cellular experiments provided some support to the tau phosphorylation hypothesis. In neuronal-like cells, muscarinic agonists reduced tau phosphorylation, a finding subsequently repeated in neurons and in transfected cells (Forlenza et al, 2000; Sadot et al, 1996). Moreover, the change in phosphorylation demonstrated in these studies is at multiple sites in tau and has the effect of altering the functional properties of tau.

Overall then these studies suggest that muscarinic agonists favourably reduce amyloidogenic metabolism and favourably reduce tau phosphorylation in cells. However, if this data held true in vivo then acetylcholinesterase inhibitors ought also to reduce tau phosphorylation and increase non-amyloidogenic APP metabolism because the effect of these compounds will be to increase the amount of acetylcholine available for postsynaptic muscarinic-receptor binding. In brain slices mimicking the intact in-vivo brain cholinesterases did increase non-amyloidogenic metabolism as expected (Mori et al, 1995) and metrifonate, an irreversible acetylcholinesterase inhibitor (ACHEI) induced non-amyloidogenic metabolism in a forebrain neurons (Pakaski et al, 2000). All of this is encouraging – it almost seems too much to hope for that drugs designed as palliative and symptomatic may have a disease-modifying effect. However, evidence of any real effect in vivo is presently lacking. Animal models and even more importantly human disease-modifying studies must be done before these in-vitro data can be taken as evidence that the cholinomimetics have an effect on the disease process.

Nicotine and nicotinic agonists

Cholinergic receptors are of two main types – muscarinic and nicotinic. Just as muscarinic agonists improve cognition in animal models so to do nicotinic compounds. Nicotine itself improves the rat's ability to find it's way around mazes (Gitelman and Prohovnik, 1992; Levin, 1992). This particular line of reasoning led to some unfortunate conclusions. First, and quite appropriately,

nicotine was explored as a potential therapy for AD. Some showed some promise with nicotine patches to deliver the compound to patients with AD (Levin and Rezvani, 2000; Wilson et al, 1995) although other studies showed little effect (Snaedal et al, 1996). In fact, the effects of nicotine in AD are most likely to be limited to attention-enhancing effects rather than the reversal of cognitive deficits intrinsic to the disease (Sahakian et al, 1989). However, the possibility of nicotine as a cognitive enhancer led some investigators to wonder whether nicotinic loss was involved in the disease, and whether smoking might be protective. Early studies suggested an inverse relation between AD and smoking (Brenner et al, 1993; Graves et al, 1991) although it was always possible that the paucity of smokers among the demented was simply because the smokers died earlier. Prospective studies have now definitively shown just this (Brenner et al, 1993; Doll et al, 2000; Graves et al, 1991), thus closing this particular chapter of AD research. Smoking protects against AD only by causing premature death.

The nicotine story itself, however, remains intriguing. Most interestingly the $\alpha7$ nicotinic receptor was shown to be the hitherto elusive amyloid receptor. Amyloid, although pathogenic in AD, is produced normally (presumably it is a relative thing – the more amyloid produced the more likely AD is to result – and relative is the appropriate word because the production of amyloid has been shown to be inherited through an as yet unidentified gene on chromosome 10). If amyloid is produced normally it should do something and so should have a receptor. This receptor appears to be the α7 receptor and amyloid binding to this receptor may stimulate some of the intracellular effects seen in AD, including tau phosphorylation (Wang et al, 2000). Nicotinic-receptor stimulation may protect against adverse effects of amyloid binding to the receptor because it protects against amyloid toxicity (Kihara et al, 1997). These results could turn out to be important because the suggestion is that the nicotinic receptor may be an important therapeutic target both to increase attention and also to reduce the adverse effects of amyloid in the brain.

Allosteric modulation of the nicotinic receptor

Binding of ligands (including nicotine and acetylcholine) to the presynaptic nicotinic receptor enhances release of acetylcholine. Thus a positive feedback is set up – release of acetylcholine primes the neuron so that if another signal is received an even greater acetylcholine release follows, the end result being increased postsynaptic cholinergic signal. Nicotine and nicotinic agonists do this as well as acetylcholine but there is another class of compounds that have the same effect. These are allosteric modulators of the

nicotinic receptor – compounds that bind to the receptor at a site distal to the nicotine-binding site but alter the primary nicotinic site to make it more sensitive. Physostigmine has weak allosteric modulation of the nicotinic receptor, galantamine, a cholinesterase inhibitor, has rather stronger effects (Maelicke, 2000). In cell and animal models it has been shown that galantamine enhances cholinergic release consistent with its pharmacological profile as an allosteric modulator of the nicotinic receptor. Whether this translates to any practical beneficial effects in humans is unknown (and difficult in principle to prove one way or another).

Other neurotransmitter systems – the case of N-methyl-D-aspartate (NMDA)

As well as loss of function of particular subsets one theory that has attracted attention for many years in AD and other neurodegenerative conditions is the possibility that over-activity of excitatory amino-acid transmitters may be related to neurotoxicity that occurs in these conditions. While there is loss of glutamergic pyramidal neurons there is no loss of glutamate binding sites – in particular NMDA receptor sites (Cowburn et al, 1990). This led to the hypothesis that a slow over-stimulation of NMDA and non-NMDA glutamate receptors may contribute to loss of neurons in AD and that this may precede the formation of amyloid plaques and other aspects of pathology (Beal, 1992). An alternative view was that neurons would be rendered more vulnerable to excitotoxic damage if exposed to amyloid, and this view was certainly substantiated by experiments in cells in culture (Gray and Patel, 1995; Mattson et al, 1992). NMDA excitotoxicity also seems to have a relation with the other component of AD pathology, because treatment of neurons with glutamate increases tau phosphorylation at the same sites as in the AD brain (Couratier et al, 1996). Moreover, glutamate increases total tau expression levels (Esclaire et al, 1997). The effect of glutamate then is to increase the amount of free tau both through increasing expression and increasing phosphorylation. It is plausible that this increase in free tau may increase tau aggregation into neurofibrillary tangles.

Because of the known neurotoxicity of excitatory amino acids a number of NMDA inhibitors have been developed for use in both chronic disorders like AD and also in acute disorders such as stroke. High-potency NMDA antagonists have unwanted psychomimetic effects but low-potency antagonists are, in general, well tolerated (Kornhuber and Weller, 1997). One such compound is Memantine which was in fact one of the first compounds to be assessed in AD (Fleischhacker et al, 1986) and has been extensively used in clinical practice in Germany (Förstl, 2000). Further evidence suggests that Memantine may be effective in advanced AD while having little interaction with cholinesterase inhibitors (Marx, 2000; Wenk et al, 2000; Winblad and Poritis, 1999). This evidence raises the exciting prospect of a novel treatment for AD that may be of use when the cholinesterase inhibitors have less effect, may be of use in combination therapy, and may be of use on a new disease target.

Summary

- The cholinesterase inhibitors have been highly successful agents in treating AD. However, other transmitter-based approaches have shown promise – not all of it realized.
- Muscarinic agonists seem to have little effect on cognition, although they and the cholinesterase inhibitors may have some effects in reducing amyloid formation and reducing tau phosphorylation.
- Nicotinic receptors agonists almost certainly increase attention and may protect against amyloid toxicity.
- Modulation of the nicotinic receptor may enhance cholinergic and other transmitter release and antagonists of the NMDA receptor may reduce neurotoxicity and be beneficial in AD.
- There is more to the neurotransmitter-based therapeutic approaches in AD than the cholinesterase inhibitors.

References

Beal MF (1992). Mechanisms of excitotoxicity in neurologic diseases. *FASEB J* **6**, 3338–44.

Bodick NC, Offen WW, Levey AI, et al (1997). Effects of xanomeline, a selective muscarinic receptor agonist, on cognitive function and behavioral symptoms in Alzheimer disease. *Arch Neurol* **54**, 465–73.

Brenner DE, Kukull WA, van Belle G, et al (1993). Relationship between cigarette smoking and Alzheimer's disease in a population-based case-control study. *Neurology* **43**, 293–300.

Couratier P, Lesort M, Sindou P, Esclaire F, Yardin C, Hugon J (1996). Modifications of neuronal phosphorylated tau immunoreactivity induced by NMDA toxicity. *Mol Chem Neuropathol* **27**, 259–73.

Cowburn RF, Hardy JA, Roberts PJ (1990). Glutamatergic neurotransmission in Alzheimer's disease. *Biochem Soc Trans* **18**, 390–92.

DeLapp N, Wu S, Belagaje R, et al (1998). Effects of the M1 agonist xanomeline on processing of human β-amyloid precursor protein (FAD, Swedish mutant) transfected into Chinese hamster ovary-m1 cells. *Biochem Biophys Res Commun* **244**, 156–60.

Doll R, Peto R, Boreham J, Sutherland I (2000). Smoking and dementia in male British doctors: prospective study. *BMJ* **320**, 1097–102.

Eckols K, Bymaster FP, Mitch CH, Shannon HE, Ward JS, DeLapp NW (1995). The muscarinic M1 agonist xanomeline increases soluble amyloid precursor protein release from Chinese hamster ovary-m1 cells. *Life Sci* **57**, 1183–90.

Esclaire F, Lesort M, Blanchard C, Hugon J (1997). Glutamate toxicity enhances tau gene expression in neuronal cultures. *J Neurosci Res* **49**, 309–18.

Fleischhacker WW, Buchgeher A, Schubert H (1986). Memantine in the treatment of senile dementia of the Alzheimer type. *Prog Neuropsychopharmacol Biol Psychiatry* **10**, 87–93.

Forlenza O, Spink J, Anderton BH, Olesen OF, Lovestone S (2000). Muscarinic agonists reduce tau phosphorylation via GSK-3 inhibition. *J Neural Transm* **107**, 1201–12.

Förstl H (2000). Clinical issues in current drug therapy for dementia. *Alzheimer Dis Assoc Disord* **14** (suppl), S103–8.

Gitelman DR, Prohovnik I (1992). Muscarinic and nicotinic contributions to cognitive function and cortical blood flow. *Neurobiol Aging* **13**, 313–18.

Graves AB, van Duijn CM, Chandra V, et al (1991). Alcohol and tobacco consumption as risk factors for Alzheimer's disease: a collaborative re-analysis of case-control studies: EURODEM Risk Factors Research Group. *Int J Epidemiol* **20** (suppl), S48–57.

Gray CW, Patel AJ (1995). Neurodegeneration mediated by glutamate and β-amyloid peptide: a comparison and possible interaction. *Brain Res* **691**, 169–79.

Greenwald BS, Davis KL (1983). Experimental pharmacology of Alzheimer disease. *Adv Neurol* **38**, 87–102.

Kihara T, Shimohama S, Sawada H, et al (1997). Nicotinic receptor stimulation protects neurons against β-amyloid toxicity. *Ann Neurol* **42**, 159–63.

Kornhuber J, Weller M (1997). Psychotogenicity and N-methyl-D-aspartate receptor antagonism: implications for neuroprotective pharmacotherapy. *Biol Psychiatry* **41**, 135–44.

Levin ED (1992). Nicotinic systems and cognitive function. *Psychopharmacology (Berl)* **108**, 417–31.

Levin ED, Rezvani AH (2000). Development of

nicotinic drug therapy for cognitive disorders. *Eur J Pharmacol* **393**, 141–46.

Little A, Levy R, Chuaqui Kidd P, Hand D (1985). A double-blind, placebo controlled trial of high-dose lecithin in Alzheimer's disease. *J Neurol Neurosurg Psychiatry* **48**, 736–42.

Maelicke A (2000). Allosteric modulation of nicotinic receptors as a treatment strategy for Alzheimer's disease. *Dementia* **11** (suppl), 11–18.

Marx J (2000). Alzheimer's congress: drug shows promise for advanced disease. *Science* **289**, 375–77.

Mattson MP, Cheng B, Davis D, Bryant K, Lieberburg I, Rydel RE (1992). Beta-amyloid peptides destabilize calcium homeostasis and render human cortical neurons vulnerable to excitotoxicity. *J Neurosci* **12**, 376–89.

Mori F, Lai CC, Fusi F, Giacobini E (1995). Cholinesterase inhibitors increase secretion of APPs in rat brain cortex. *Neuroreport* **6**, 633–36.

Muller D, Wiegmann H, Langer U, Moltzen-Lenz S, Nitsch RM (1998). Lu 25-109, a combined m1 agonist and m2 antagonist, modulates regulated processing of the amyloid precursor protein of Alzheimer's disease. *J Neural Transm* **105**, 1029–43.

Pakaski M, Rakonczay Z, Fakla I, Papp H, Kasa P (2000). In vitro effects of metrifonate on neuronal amyloid precursor protein processing and protein kinase C level. *Brain Res* **863**, 266–70.

Raffaele KC, Berardi A, Asthana S, Morris P, Haxby JV, Soncrant TT (1991). Effects of long-term continuous infusion of the muscarinic cholinergic agonist arecoline on verbal memory in dementia of the Alzheimer type. *Psychopharmacol Bull* **27**, 315–19.

Sadot E, Gurwitz D, Barg J, Behar L, Ginzburg I, Fisher A (1996). Activation of m1 muscarinic acetylcholine receptor regulates tau phosphorylation in transfected PC12 cells. *J Neurochem* **66**, 877–80.

Sahakian B, Jones G, Levy R, Gray J, Warburton D (1989). The effects of nicotine on attention, information processing, and short-term memory in patients with dementia of the Alzheimer type. *Br J Psychiatry* **154**, 797–800.

Snaedal J, Johannesson T, Jonsson JE, Gylfadottir G (1996). The effects of nicotine in dermal plaster on cognitive functions in patients with Alzheimer's disease. *Dementia* **7**, 47–52.

Thal LJ, Forrest M, Loft H, Mengel H, Lu 25-109 Study Group (2000). Lu 25-109, a muscarinic agonist, fails to improve cognition in Alzheimer's disease. *Neurology* **54**, 421–26.

Veroff AE, Bodick NC, Offen WW, Sramek JJ, Cutler NR (1998). Efficacy of xanomeline in Alzheimer disease: cognitive improvement measured using the Computerized Neuropsychological Test Battery (CNTB). *Alzheimer Dis Assoc Disord* **12**, 304–12.

Wang HY, Lee DHS, Davis CB, Shank RP (2000). Amyloid peptide $A\beta_{1-42}$ binds selectively and with picomolar affinity to $\alpha 7$ nicotinic acetylcholine receptors. *J Neurochem* **75**, 1155–61.

Wenk GL, Quack G, Moebius HJ, Danysz W (2000). No interaction of memantine with acetylcholinesterase inhibitors approved for clinical use. *Life Sci* **66**, 1079–83.

Wilson AL, Langley LK, Monley J, et al (1995). Nicotine patches in Alzheimer's disease: pilot study on learning, memory, and safety. *Pharmacol Biochem Behav* **51**, 509–14.

Winblad B, Poritis N (1999). Memantine in severe dementia: results of the 9M-Best Study (benefit and efficacy in severely demented patients during treatment with memantine). *Int J Geriatr Psychiatry* **14**, 135–46.

Disease modification

8

The revolution in treatment of Alzheimer's disease (AD) of the acetylcholin esterase inhibitor (ACHEI) is all very well, but they were designed as symptomatic treatments and, ultimately, therapies that are truly useful in AD will be disease-modifying. Where will such therapies come from? Serendipity is usually the answer but rationally designed disease-modification strategies are likely to rise out of two broad scientific approaches to understanding AD – molecular pathogenesis and epidemiology.

Possible disease modification strategies from molecular pathogenesis

The understanding of the pathology of AD, while not complete, can now be described in some detail. Essentially the amyloid cascade hypothesis proposed by Hardy and Higgins (1992) is correct. As originally stated this hypothesis proposes that amyloid deposition is at the core of AD pathology (as well as in the core of plaques) and that the other signs of AD including the accumulation of highly phosphorylated tau in neurofibrillary tangles in neurons, the loss of neurons and the subsequent atrophy and clinical symptoms, all result as a consequence of amyloid deposition. The amyloid-cascade hypothesis has had some modifications – it may be intercellular amyloid that is important and it may be necessary for tau to accumulate in tangles (as opposed to this being an epiphenomenon) – but it has nonetheless been substantiated by almost every single important discovery subsequently. Just to mention a few of these discoveries: all the mutations in different genes that cause early-onset AD result in altered amyloid-precursor-protein (APP) metabolism and increased amyloid production; the gene associated with late-onset AD, APOE, also binds to and probably affects amyloid; animals harbouring APP mutations, and even more so those with both APP and presenilin-1 mutations, have amyloid deposits and some have cognitive deficits as well. While there are still some unexplained observations the amyloid-cascade hypothesis is the most likely explanation for the pathological events that occur in AD (see Figure 8.1). It is unclear how amyloid induces tau phosphorylation; it is possible that tau aggregation could precede phosphorylation and it is conceivable (and fiercely argued) that amyloid itself may result in cognitive impairment and/or neuronal loss. However, despite these unresolved matters the scheme shown in figure 8.1 illustrates all of the obvious disease-modification strategies that have arisen out of the molecular biology of AD.

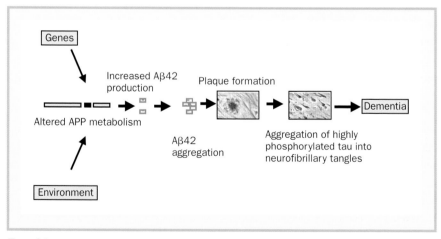

Figure 8.1
The amyloid cascade hypothesis of Alzheimer's disease pathogenesis – each of the steps illustrated is a target for disease modification.

Altering amyloid

APP is cleaved by at least three secretase activities. Sequential cleavage by β-secretase followed by γ-secretase generates the amyloid moiety whereas cleavage by α-secretase cuts APP within the amyloid sequence. Each of these enzymes then becomes a target for disease-modifying therapy. Inhibition of β-secretase or γ-secretase would be protective as would enhancement of the activity of α-secretase. A huge international effort generated a fierce race to discover β-secretase, which was finally revealed in October 1999 and re-named beta-site APP-cleaving enzyme or BACE (Vassar et al, 1999). It is certain that inhibitors of this enzyme will be found and examined for therapeutic benefits. γ-Secretase is a more difficult target because increasing evidence suggests that γ-secretase is in fact another AD gene – presenilin-1 (Annaert et al, 1999; De Strooper et al, 1999). Presenilin-1 also cleaves other proteins including Notch, which is involved in haematopoesis. Inhibition of γ-secretase may well have unwanted and dangerous effects. Nonetheless, inhibitors of γ-secretase will surely be sought and tested for disease modification.

Inhibition of an action of an enzyme is generally easier than enhancement of it. However, it is possible that enhancement of the action of α-secretase could be achieved. Although not yet identified, this enzyme is one of a class that is stimulated by the second messenger protein kinase C (PKC). Stimulating PKC in cells and animals has been shown to stimulate α-secretase cleavage of APP and in some cases to reduce amyloid production (Benussi et al, 1998; Gabuzda et al, 1993; Racchi et al, 1999). PKC is itself stimulated by a variety of neurotransmitters including certain (m1/m3) muscarinic receptors. This would suggest that M1 agonists would reduce amyloid and/or increase non-amyloidogenic processing of APP and indeed in model systems this is exactly what has been found (DeLapp et al, 1998; Nitsch et al, 1993; Nitsch et al, 1996). This exciting finding suggests that any strategy that increases m1 receptor activity, including both m1 agonists and ACHEIs, would have disease-modifying effects (reviewed in Lovestone, 1997).

Finally, it is still not known what is pathogenic about amyloid or, more accurately, in what form is amyloid pathogenic. Is it soluble amyloid peptide, soluble amyloid oligomers, or aggregated and fibrillised amyloid? One hypothesis is that it is the aggregated fibrillised amyloid that is pathogenic. There is quite good evidence for this from cell biology because amyloid peptide has to be aged in the test-tube to be neurotoxic and this ageing is accompanied by fibrillation. This assay provides an excellent means to search for compounds that prevent fibrillation. Patents have been filed on a number of such agents, which presumably are in development as disease-modification therapies.

The most remarkable potential therapy, however, comes from the observation that immunization of transgenic animals against amyloid stimulates an immune response that may be therapeutic. Animals that overexpress APP carrying the mutation that causes familial AD acquire some of the features of the disease including amyloid plaques. When amyloid itself was injected into these animals they developed an immune response and the numbers of plaques dramatically reduced (Schenk et al, 1999). This is a quite extraordinary finding – perhaps the most remarkable in all AD research. Further work (Bard et al, 2000) shows that passive immunization with antibody has the same effect and that cognitive deficits are reduced. Not surprisingly human trials started within months of this finding being reported.

Targeting tau

The importance of tau to the pathology of dementia came with genetic discoveries (as it so often does). Highly phosphorylated tau, a microtubule-associated protein, essential for normal neuronal functioning, aggregates in neurofibrillary tangles in AD and in other dementias. The phosphorylation of tau reduces its normal function by reducing its binding to tangles (reviewed in Lovestone and Reynolds, 1997). For many years, however,

the importance of this to AD was disputed until it was shown that some forms of frontal-lobe dementia are caused by mutations in tau and that these mutations also reduce its ability to bind to microtubules (Dayanandan et al, 1999; Hutton et al, 1998). This finding suggested the scheme in Figure 8.2 where phosphorylation reduces tau binding to its normal substrate, increasing its ability to bind to itself and thereby resulting in loss of normal function in the neuron and loss of normal microtubules.

Two sites of intervention are suggested by this scheme – prevention of aggregation and prevention of phosphorylation. Tau aggregation inhibitors have not yet been identified but some of the factors that enhance tau aggregation have been demonstrated and so such compounds are certainly feasible (Hasegawa et al, 1997). Phosphorylation of tau may be a better or at least more immediate target. Tau is phosphorylated by several enzymes but we have shown in cells that only one of these is any good at phosphorylating tau in the same way as in AD brain – an enzyme called GSK-3 (Lovestone et al, 1994). Inhibition of GSK-3 in neurons reduces tau phosphorylation (Hong et al, 1997; Hong and Lee 1997), suggesting that this may be a feasible strategy. One very strong inhibitor of GSK-3 is known – lithium. At therapeutic concentrations lithium inhibits GSK-3, it inhibits GSK-3 in neurons, reduces tau phosphorylation, and restores the normal

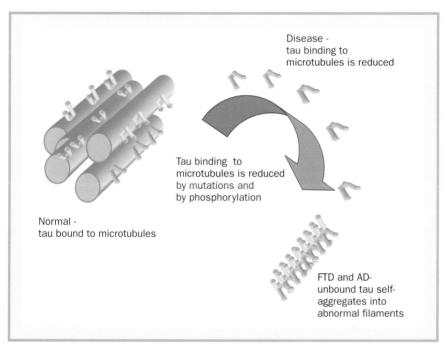

Figure 8.2
The formation of paired helical filaments from the microtubule associated protein tau.

function of tau (Hong et al, 1997; Leroy et al, 2000; Lovestone et al, 1999). Two interesting and tantalising consequences arise – could lithium be protective against AD and could this be the action of lithium in bipolar disorder? These are testable suggestions.

GSK-3 is also inhibited by PKC and this would suggest that activation PKC would be protective and reduce tau phosphorylation. We have discussed this above in relation to APP – muscarinic agonists increase PKC activity and increase non-amyloidogenic metabolism. Would the same compounds do the same for tau? Indeed, this appears to be the case and muscarinic agonists reduce tau phosphorylation, do so in non-neuronal cells, neuroblastoma cells, and in neurons and improves the function of tau as they do so (Forlenza et al, 2000; Sadot et al, 1996). Increase in cholinergic function therefore improves cognition, and in model systems, at least, increases non-amyloidogenic APP metabolism and reduces tau phosphorylation. Such a remarkable set of properties suggests a common pathophysiological link (Francis et al, 1999; Lovestone, 1997).

Possible disease-modification strategies from epidemiology

Limiting inflammation

It is a curious observation that at the same time that molecular biologists were demonstrating that the immune response generated by amyloid injection may be therapeutic (Schenk et al, 1999), epidemiologists were showing that anti-inflammatory drugs were protective (Andersen et al, 1995; Breitner et al, 1995; Delanty and Vaughan, 1998). These observations were first made in case-control studies that showed that those receiving non-steroidal anti-inflammatory drugs (NSAIDs) for other indications, including leprosy and arthritis, had less AD than expected. Both case-control and prospective studies with Alzheimer populations have tended to confirm these observations. NSAIDs and Cox-2 inhibitors are undergoing prospective assessment as protective strategies. However, the vaccinated mouse story strongly suggests that not all inflammation is harmful and there may be selective effects both temporally (ie, early

reduction in inflammation may prevent amyloid generation, late inflammation may help to remove amyloid once formed) and physiologically (ie, some components of inflammation may be beneficial, others harmful).

Reducing oxidation

There is a lot of evidence for oxidative stress in AD (Markesbery, 1999; Markesbery and Carney, 1999). Despite the molecular biology and epidemiology advances, age remains the most obvious and important risk factor for AD and oxidative damage is an inevitable consequence of age. Free radicals are generated in most metabolic processes and damage due to free radicals, including lipid peridoxation, increases with age (Butterfield et al, 1999; Münch et al, 1997). Amyloid itself may generate free radicals and there is convincing evidence that the toxicity of amyloid, at least in model systems, is reduced by antioxidants (Aksenov et al, 1998; Bozner et al, 1997; Café et al, 1996; Suo et al, 1997; Thomas et al, 1996). All these data suggest that antioxidants may have disease-modifying effects. Potential antioxidants include vitamin E and vitamin C, idebenone, and perhaps MAO-B inhibitors such as selegiline (because MAO-B increases in the free-radical generating astrocytes). Vitamin E has been subjected to clinical trial and shows some beneficial effects in increasing time to nursing home care (Sano et al, 1997). However, the doses used were very large and patients taking the recommend dose as a dietary supplement are almost certainly not having any substantial antioxidant effect (compared with that achieved in the trial). Further trials of vitamin E are needed before it can be recommended.

Replacing hormones

A series of epidemiology studies (eg, Paganini-Hill and Henderson, 1994) suggested that women receiving hormone-replacement therapy were at less risk of suffering AD. The biological basis behind such an observation is not known but a variety of plausible suggestions have been made (Birge, 1997; Paganini-Hill and Henderson, 1994). However, it should be noted that not all the epidemiology points in the same direction (Brenner et al, 1994). Despite this a series of trials have attempted to replace oestrogen as a disease-modifying strategy. The published work was reviewed by Haskell et al (1997) who identified 19 studies including ten randomized trials of replacement therapy. Of these randomized trials, eight claimed therapeutic benefits in memory or attention but did not control for factors such as depression. The observational studies are obviously less valuable but nonetheless five found a significant association between oestrogen use and cognitive function. Haskell

et al (1997) concluded that these studies provide some encouragement but the defining studies will be the large multi-centre randomized controlled trials currently underway.

Reducing vascular disease and diabetes

The distinction between vascular dementia and AD is one of the defining features of the clinical process, but has been challenged by evidence that the distinction between the two conditions may not be as great as once supposed. In fact mixed dementia may be the most common dementia and is certainly more common than vascular dementia alone (Holmes et al, 1999). Moreover, there is some evidence that vascular risk factors may be independent risk factors for AD (Breteler et al, 1998; Skoog et al, 1999). It follows that prevention of vascular risk factors – reducing blood pressure, reducing atherosclereosis – may be of some use in prevention of dementia. Whether the same measures, or others such as aspirin, could have a role in disease modification remains to be seen.

As plasma total homocysteine is a risk factor for vascular disease it could also be a risk factor for AD or other dementias. In a case-control study serum homocysteine was associated with AD with an odds ratio of 4.5 for the top third homocysteine levels in the AD group compared with the bottom third of the control group was 4.5; serum folate and B12 levels were correspondingly lower in the AD group than controls (Clarke et al, 1998). These are interesting findings and deserve replication before folate/B12 replacement therapy is considered a useful disease-modifying therapy.

Diabetes has also been associated with AD (reviewed in Stewart and Liolitsa, 1999). The mechanism whereby diabetes could increase risk is unclear, particularly since insulin resistance is also associated with risk (Kuusisto et al, 1997), suggesting that it is not via the proxy of vascular complications of diabetes (Lovestone, 1999). Because insulin reduces tau phosphorylation (Hong and Lee, 1997) and also increases non-amyloidogenic metabolism of APP (Solano et al, 2000) this suggests that a signalling defect may underlie the association. Effective treatment of diabetes may be disease modifying but only if the signalling cascade is intact. In the largest prospective study showing that diabetes was associated with AD those patients on insulin actually had higher risk (Ott et al, 1999). This suggests that the association with diabetes shown by epidemiology may be of more use to the molecular biologists looking for new treatments rather than the public-health clinicians aiming to reduce risk factors.

Disease-modification trial designs

Molecular biology and epidemiology are generating targets for disease modification. But how are attempts to hit these targets be assessed? For a disease that in which the person deteriorates relentlessly, to distinguish between symptomatic treatment and disease modification is not simple. The first steps in attempts at modification of AD progression, and the scientific measurement of such modification, have been to understand its natural history, and then to develop outcomes appropriate to the stage of disease that is targeted for therapy. Outcomes for early-stage disease are different from those for late-onset disease. Outcomes used have included cognition, function, and time to disease stage. Brain imaging has now been added as a valuable surrogate outcome.

The study of the natural history of AD has been facilitated by clinical research criteria such as the DSM-IV and the NINCDS-ADRDA criteria (McKhann et al, 1984). Some longitudinal studies spanning from 1–7 years have looked at annual changes in cognition and functional autonomy (Katzman et al, 1988; Lucca et al, 1993; Morris et al, 1993; Mortimer et al, 1992) or at cumulative rates of nursing-home placement and death (Berg et al, 1988; Bracco et al, 1994; Heyman et al, 1996; Heyman et al, 1997; Stern et al, 1997). Clinical milestones have been described in AD (Panel 8.1), some potentially useful as endpoints for randomized clinical trials (Galasko et al, 1995).

In clinical practice, patients with typical AD followed over the expected survival time of 8 years (Barclay et al, 1985) will often show anxiety and depression early in their evolution, and neuropsychiatric manifestations will emerge at the intermediate stage, to abate in the late stage where motor signs become prominent (Sclan et al, 1996). Cognitive and functional decline tend to be more linear, whereas caregiver burden peaks and decreases in parallel to the neuropsychiatric symptoms (Zarit et al, 1986).

Designs of randomized clinical trials designs to prove delay in progression have been reviewed critically (Bodick et al, 1997; Gauthier, 1998; Gauthier et al, 1996; Whitehouse et al, 1998; Panel 8.2). The 1 year parallel-groups design has been used more widely so far, with negative results with

Panel 8.1
Clinical milestones in AD

- conversion from mild cognitive impairment to dementia
- loss of selected ADLs
- emergence of neuropsychiatric symptoms
- nursing-home placement
- loss of self-care ADLs
- death

Panel 8.2
Study designs for disease modification

- parallel groups over 1 year or longer
- survival to reaching the next milestone(s)
- staggered start and withdrawal
- single-blind or double-blind active drug withdrawal
- open-label extended follow-up

prednisone (Aisen et al, 2000) and estrogens (Henderson et al, 2000) versus placebo, but there is great interest in the time to reach clinical milestones or survival design, as shown by the very high clinical impact of the Sano et al (1997) study to compare tocopherol with selegiline and placebo. The staggered-start/withdrawal design had originally been suggested by Leber (1997) but has proven to be difficult to apply, because of the high attrition of patients over time. A single-blind drug washout component to trials has been useful to show the reversibility of donepezil action over 6 weeks (Doody and Pratt, 1999), and it is postulated that an agent slowing disease progression would have shown a lack of reversibility during such a washout period. Data from open-label extensions of trials suggest a sustained 'shift to the right' or sustained therapeutic benefit over many months (Raskind et al, 2000; Rogers and Friedhoff, 1998), but lack a control group.

There are thus differences in intensity and type of symptoms at each stage of AD, and cognitive as well as functional decline tend to be more linear over time than mood and behavioural symptoms. Similarly the rating scales may not be perfectly linear over time. For instance, outcome variables to measure cognitive decline such as the Alzheimer's Disease Assessment Scale – cognitive (Rosen et al, 1984) and the Mini Mental State Examination (Folstein et al, 1975) are sigmoidal, with an initial plateau phase, a steep phase, and a floor effect between moderate and severe stages of AD (Kertesz and Mohs, 1999). Some activities of daily living (ADL) scales are specific towards instrumental tasks (IADL), which are lost early in the course of AD and generally not reversible, whereas others measure self-care ADL which are lost in later stages (Gélinas and Auer, 2001).

The decision to study a disease-modification effect on patients at a given stage (from mild to severe AD) will thus clearly influence the choice of outcome variables and possibly the trial design itself and its duration. For instance, in the mild stage of AD, there is little cognitive loss over 1 year, some loss of IADL but no loss in self-care ADL, and few neuropsychiatric symptoms will emerge. In the moderate stage there will be a more rapid decline in cognition, in both IADL and self-care ADL, and in behaviour as reported by family members. In severe stage, cognitive instruments such as Severe Impairment Battery (Panisset et al, 1994) will be more

sensitive to change, and behaviour can be observed by formal caregivers in institutions.

Given the symptomatic benefit of cholinesterase inhibitors (CI) in many patients the new issue of whether placebo-controlled randomized clinical trials are still possible in mild-to-moderate stages of AD has arisen, with arguments for (Farlow, 1998; Karlawish and Whitehouse, 1998) and against (Knopman et al, 1998). There are no ethical restrictions at present against placebo studies in AD (Post, 1998), but there may well be practical ones. The enrollment of 'non-responders' to CIs may become necessary in trials that aim to delaying progression, alternatively all patients will be treated as 'usual care' that would include a CI and possibly vitamin E.

A novel design has been proposed by Petersen et al (1999), consisting of the conversion from mild cognitive impairment to diagnosable AD. There are currently a number of trials looking at the potential preventive effects of Cox-2 selective inhibitors, tocopherol, and CI such as donepezil, rivastigmine, and galantamine, versus placebo. The validity of these studies may be enhanced by the addition of brain volumetric measurements on MRI scans (Rombouts et al, 2000), which would show a slower rate of whole brain or regional atrophy in patients who are on active treatment versus those on placebo.

Summary

- Epidemiology and molecular biology have suggested many targets for therapy. Strategies currently under consideration include decreasing amyloidogenic metabolism or increasing non-amyloidogenic metabolism, reducing amyloid aggregation or reducing tau phosphorylation or aggregation.
- Epidemiology also has suggested targets including anti-inflammatory, hormone replacement, anti-oxidant and anti-vascular risk strategies.
- Measurement of the effects of any of these strategies will not be straightforward. The natural history of Alzheimer's disease consists of a steady decline through a sequence of clinical milestones, mild cognitive impairment, to loss of functional autonomy, neuropsychiatric manifestations, and need for institutionalization.
- Delaying progression from mild cognitive impairment to diagnosable AD and from mild-to-severe stages of AD are valuable therapeutic goals and could be achieved by modifications of primary or secondary pathological features of the disease.
- Randomized clinical trials of at least 1 year duration are required to test these treatment hypotheses, aiming at changing slopes in the decline of a given variable, or delaying the time to reach a specific milestone.

References

Aisen PS, Davis KL, Berg JD, et al (2000). A randomized controlled trial of prednisone in Alzheimer's disease. *Neurology* 54, 588–93.

Aksenov MY, Aksenova MV, Markesbery WR, Butterfield DA (1998). Amyloid β-peptide(1–40)-mediated oxidative stress in cultured hippocampal neurons – protein carbonyl formation, CK BB expression, and the level of Cu, Zn, and Mn SOD mRNA. *J Mol Neurosci* 10, 181–92.

Andersen K, Launer LJ, Ott A, Hoes AW, Breteler MMB, Hofman A (1995). Do nonsteroidal anti-inflammatory drugs decrease the risk for Alzheimer's disease? The Rotterdam Study. *Neurology* 45, 1441–45.

Annaert WG, Levesque L, Craessaerts K, et al (1999). Presenilin 1 controls gamma-secretase processing of amyloid precursor protein in pre-Golgi compartments of hippocampal neurons. *J Cell Biol* 147, 277–94.

Barclay LL, Zemcov A, Blass JP, Sansone J (1985). Survival in Alzheimer's disease and vascular dementias. *Neurology* 35, 834–40.

Bard F, Cannon C, Barbour R, et al (2000). Peripherally administered antibodies against amyloid beta-peptide enter the central nervous system and reduce pathology in a mouse model of Alzheimer disease. *Nat Med* 6, 916-19

Benussi L, Govoni S, Gasparini L, et al (1998). Specific role for protein kinase Cα in the constitutive and regulated secretion of amyloid precursor protein in human skin fibroblasts. *Neurosci Lett* 240, 97–101.

Berg L, Miller JP, Storandt M, et al (1988). Mild

senile dementia of the Alzheimer type: 2. Longitudinal assessment. *Ann Neurol* **23**, 477–84.

Birge SJ (1997). The role of estrogen in the treatment of Alzheimer's disease. *Neurology* **48** (suppl), S36–41.

Bodick N, Forette F, Hadler D, et al (1997). Protocols to demonstrate slowing of Alzheimer disease progression – position paper from the International Working Group on Harmonization of Dementia Drug Guidelines. *Alzheimer Dis Assoc Disord* **11** (suppl), 50–53.

Bozner P, Grishko V, LeDoux SP, Wilson GL, Chyan YC, Pappolla MA (1997). The amyloid β protein induces oxidative damage of mitochondrial DNA. *J Neuropathol Exp Neurol* **56**, 1356–62.

Bracco L, Gallato R, Grigoletto F, et al (1994). Factors affecting course and survival in Alzheimer's disease: a 9–year longitudinal study. *Arch Neurol* **51**, 1213–19.

Breitner JC, Welsh KA, Helms MJ, et al (1995). Delayed onset of Alzheimer's disease with nonsteroidal anti-inflammatory and histamine H2 blocking drugs. *Neurobiol Aging* **16**, 523–30.

Brenner DE, Kukull WA, Stergachis A, et al (1994). Postmenopausal estrogen replacement therapy and the risk of Alzheimer's disease: a population-based case-control study. *Am J Epidemiol* **140**, 262–67.

Breteler MMB, Bots ML, Ott A, Hofman A (1998). Risk factors for vascular disease and dementia. *Haemostasis* **28**, 167–73.

Butterfield DA, Howard B, Yatin S, et al (1999). Elevated oxidative stress in models of normal brain aging and Alzheimer's disease. *Life Sci* **65**, 1883–92.

Café C, Torri C, Bertorelli L, et al (1996). Oxidative stress after acute and chronic application of β-amyloid fragment 25–35 in cortical cultures. *Neurosci Lett* **203**, 61–65.

Dayanandan R, Van Slegtenhorst M, Mack TG, et al (1999). Mutations in tau reduce its microtubule binding properties in intact cells and affect its phosphorylation. *FEBS Lett* **446**, 228–32.

De Strooper B, Annaert W, Cupers P, et al (1999). A presenilin-1-dependent gamma-secretase-like protease mediates release of Notch intracellular domain. *Nature* **398**, 518–22.

Delanty N, Vaughan C (1998). Risk of Alzheimer's disease and duration of NSAID use. *Neurology* **51**, 652.

DeLapp N, Wu S, Belagaje R, et al (1998). Effects of the M1 agonist xanomeline on processing of human β-amyloid precursor protein (FAD, Swedish mutant) transfected into Chinese hamster ovary-m1 cells. *Biochem Biophys Res Commun* **244**, 156–60.

Doody RS, Pratt RD (1999). Clinical benefits of donepezil: results from a long-term phase III extension trial. *Neurology* **52** (suppl), A174.

Farlow MR (1998). New treatments in Alzheimer disease and the continued need for placebo-controlled trials. *Arch Neurol* **55**, 1396–98.

Folstein MF, Folstein SE, McHugh PR (1975). Mini-Mental State: a practical method of grading the cognitive state of patients for the clinician. *J Psychiatr Res* **12**, 189–98.

Forlenza O, Spink J, Anderton BH, Olesen OF, Lovestone S (2000). Muscarinic agonists reduce tau phosphorylation via GSK-3 inhibition. *J Neural Transm* **107**, 1201-12.

Francis PT, Palmer AM, Snape M, Wilcock GK (1999). The cholinergic hypothesis of Alzheimer's disease: a review of progress. *J Neurol Neurosurg Psychiatry* **66**, 137–47.

Gabuzda D, Busciglio J, Yankner BA (1993).

Inhibition of β-amyloid production by activation of protein kinase C. *J Neurochem* **61**, 2326–29.

Galasko D, Edland SD, Morris JC, Clark C, Mohs R, Koss E (1995). The Consortium to Establish a Registry for Alzheimer's Disease (CERAD) – Part XI. Clinical milestones in patients with Alzheimer's disease followed over 3 years. *Neurology* **45**, 1451–55.

Gauthier S (1998). Clinical trials and therapy. *Curr Op Neurol* **11**, 435–38.

Gauthier S, Poirier J, Gray J (1996). Effects on decline or deterioration. In: Becker R, Giacobini E, eds, *Alzheimer's disease: from molecular biology to therapy*. Boston: Birkhäuser Boston, 381–85.

Gélinas I, Auer S (2001). Functional autonomy. In: Gauthier S, ed, *Clinical diagnosis and management of Alzheimer's disease*, 2nd rev edn. London: Martin Dunitz, 191–202.

Hardy JA, Higgins GA (1992). Alzheimer's disease: the amyloid cascade hypothesis. *Science* **256**, 184–85.

Hasegawa M, Crowther RA, Jakes B, Goedert M (1997). Alzheimer-like changes in microtubule-associated protein tau induced by sulfated glycosaminoglycans – inhibition of microtubule binding, stimulation of phosphorylation, and filament assembly depend on the degree of sulfation. *J Biol Chem* **272**, 33118–24.

Haskell SG, Richardson ED, Horwitz RI (1997). The effect of estrogen replacement therapy on cognitive function in women: a critical review of the literature. *J Clin Epidemiol* **50**, 1249–64.

Henderson VW, Paganini-Hill A, Miller BL, et al. (2000). Estrogen for Alzheimer's disease in women – randomized, double-blind, placebo-controlled trial. *Neurology* **54**, 295–301.

Heyman A, Peterson B, Fillenbaum G, Pieper C (1996). The consortium to establish a registry for Alzheimer's disease (CERAD): 14.

Demographic and clinical predictors of survival in patients with Alzheimer's. *Neurology* **46**, 656–60.

Heyman A, Peterson B, Fillenbaum G, Pieper C (1997). Predictors of time to institutionalization of patients with Alzheimer's disease: The CERAD experience 17. *Neurology* **48**, 1304–9.

Holmes C, Cairns N, Lantos P, Mann A (1999). Validity of current clinical criteria for Alzheimer's disease, vascular dementia and dementia with Lewy bodies. *Br J Psychiatry* **174**, 45–50.

Hong M, Chen DC, Klein PS, Lee VM (1997). Lithium reduces tau phosphorylation by inhibition of glycogen synthase kinase-3. *J Biol Chem* **272**, 25326–32.

Hong M, Lee VMY (1997). Insulin and insulin-like growth factor-1 regulate tau phosphorylation in cultured human neurons. *J Biol Chem* **272**, 19547–53.

Hutton M, Lendon CL, Rizzu P, et al (1998). Association of missense and 5'-splice-site mutations in tau with the inherited dementia FTDP-17. *Nature* **393**, 702–5.

Karlawish JH, Whitehouse PJ (1998). Is the placebo control obsolete in a world after donepezil and vitamin E? *Arch Neurol* **55**, 1420–24.

Katzman R, Brown T, Thal LJ, et al (1988). Comparison of rate of annual change of mental status score in four independent studies of patients with Alzheimer's disease. *Ann Neurol* **24**, 384–89.

Kertesz A, Mohs R (1999). Cognition. In: Gauthier S, ed, *Clinical diagnosis and management of Alzheimer's disease*, 2nd edn. London: Martin Dunitz, 179–96.

Knopman D, Kahn J, Miles S (1998). Clinical research designs for emerging treatments for Alzheimer disease – moving beyond placebo-controlled trials. *Arch Neurol* **55**, 1425–29.

Kuusisto J, Koivisto K, Mykkänen L, et al (1997). Association between features of the insulin resistance syndrome and Alzheimer's disease independently of apolipoprotein E4 phenotype: cross sectional population based study. *BMJ* **315**, 1045–49.

Leber P (1997). Slowing the progression of Alzheimer disease: methodologic issues. *Alzheimer Dis Assoc Disord* **11** (suppl), S10–20.

Leroy K, Menu R, Conreur JL, et al (2000). The function of the microtubule-associated protein tau is variably modulated by graded changes in glycogen synthase kinase-3β activity. *FEBS Lett* **465**, 34–38.

Lovestone S (1997). Muscarinic therapies in Alzheimer's disease: from palliative therapies to disease modification. *Int J Psychiatr Clin Pract* **1**, 15–20.

Lovestone S (1999). Diabetes and dementia: is the brain another site of end-organ damage? *Neurology* **53**, 1907–9.

Lovestone S, Davis DR, Webster MT, et al (1999). Lithium reduces tau phosphorylation – effects in living cells and in neurons at therapeutic concentrations. *Biol Psychiatry* **45**, 995–1003.

Lovestone S, Reynolds CH (1997). The phosphorylation of tau: a critical stage in neurodevelopmental and neurodegenerative processes. *Neuroscience* **78**, 309–24.

Lovestone S, Reynolds CH, Latimer D, et al (1994). Alzheimer's disease-like phosphorylation of the microtubule-associated protein tau by glycogen synthase kinase-3 in transfected mammalian cells. *Curr Biol* **4**, 1077–86.

Lucca U, Comelli M, Tettamanti M, Tiraboschi P, Spagnoli A (1993). Rate of progression and prognostic factors in Alzheimer's disease: a prospective study. *J Am Geriatr Soc* **41**, 45–49.

Markesbery WR (1999). The role of oxidative stress in Alzheimer disease. *Arch Neurol* **56**, 1449–52.

Markesbery WR, Carney JM (1999). Oxidative alterations in Alzheimer's disease. *Brain Pathology* **9**, 133–46.

McKhann G, Drachman D, Folstein M, Katzman R, Price D, Stadlan EM (1984). Clinical diagnosis of Alzheimer's disease: report of the NINCDS-ADRDA work group under the auspices of Department of Health and Human Services Task Force on Alzheimer's Disease. *Neurology* **34**, 939–44.

Morris JC, Edland S, Clark C, et al (1993). The consortium to establish a registry for Alzheimer's disease (CERAD): Part IV. Rates of cognitive change in the longitudinal assessment of probable Alzheimer's disease. *Neurology* **43**, 2457–65.

Mortimer JA, Ebbitt B, Jun SP, Finch MD (1992). Predictors of cognitive and functional progression in patients with probable Alzheimer's disease. *Neurology* **42**, 1689–96.

Münch G, Thome J, Foley P, Schinzel R, Riederer P (1997). Advanced glycation endproducts in ageing and Alzheimer's disease. *Brain Res Rev* **23**, 134–43.

Nitsch RM, Slack BE, Farber SA, et al (1993). Receptor-coupled amyloid precursor protein processing. *Ann NY Acad Sci* **695**, 122–27.

Nitsch RM, Wurtman RJ, Growdon JH (1996). Regulation of APP processing – potential for the therapeutical reduction of brain amyloid burden. *Ann NY Acad Sci* **777**, 175–82.

Ott A, Stolk RP, van Harskamp F, Pols HA, Hofman A, Breteler MM (1999). Diabetes mellitus and the risk of dementia: the Rotterdam Study. *Neurology* **53**, 1937–42.

Paganini-Hill A, Henderson VW (1994). Estrogen deficiency and risk of Alzheimer's disease in women. *Am J Epidemiol* **140**, 256–61.

Panisset M, Roudier M, Saxton J, Boller F (1994). Severe impairment battery: a neuropsychological test for severely demented patients. *Arch Neurol* 51, 41–45.

Petersen RC, Smith GE, Waring SC, Ivnik RJ, Tangalos EG, Kokmen E (1999). Mild cognitive impairment: clinical characterization and outcome. *Arch Neurol* 56, 303–8. (Published erratum in *Arch Neurol* 1999 56: 760.)

Post S (1998). Societal and ethical considerations. In: Gauthier S, ed, *Pharmacotherapy of Alzheimer's disease*, London: Martin Dunitz, 113–22.

Racchi M, Solano DC, Sironi M, Govoni S (1999). Activity of α-secretase as the common final effector of protein kinase C-dependent and -independent modulation of amyloid precursor protein metabolism. *J Neurochem* 72, 2464–70.

Raskind MA, Peskind ER, Wessel T, Yuan W (2000). Galantamine in AD: a 6-month randomized, placebo-controlled trial with a 6-month extension. *Neurology* 54, 2261–68.

Rogers SL, Friedhoff LT (1998). Long-term efficacy and safety of donepezil in the treatment of Alzheimer's disease: an interim analysis of the results of a US multicentre open label extension study. *Eur Neuropsychopharmacol* 8, 67–75.

Rombouts SA, Barkhof F, Witter MP, Scheltens P (2000). Unbiased whole-brain analysis of gray matter loss in Alzheimer's disease. *Neurosci Lett* 285, 231–33.

Rosen WG, Mohs RC, Davis KL (1984). A new rating scale for Alzheimer's disease. *Am J Psychiatry* 141, 1356–64.

Sadot E, Gurwitz D, Barg J, Behar L, Ginzburg I, Fisher A (1996). Activation of m1 muscarinic acetylcholine receptor regulates tau phosphorylation in transfected PC12 cells. *J Neurochem* 66, 877–80.

Sano M, Ernesto C, Thomas RG, et al (1997b). A controlled trial of selegiline, alpha-tocopherol, or both as treatment for Alzheimer's disease. the Alzheimer's Disease Cooperative Study. *N Engl J Med* 336, 1216–22.

Schenk D, Barbour R, Dunn W, et al (1999). Immunization with amyloid-beta attenuates Alzheimer-disease-like pathology in the PDAPP mouse. *Nature* 400, 173–77.

Sclan SG, Saillon A, Franssen E, et al (1996). The behavior pathology in Alzheimer's disease rating scale (Behave-AD): reliability and analysis of symptom category scores. *Int J Geriatr Psychiatr* 11, 819–30.

Skoog I, Kalaria RN, Breteler MMB (1999) Vascular factors and Alzheimer disease. *Alzheimer Dis Assoc Disord* 13 (suppl), S106–14.

Solano DC, Sironi M, Bonfini C, Solerte SB, Govoni S, Racchi M (2000). Insulin regulates soluble amyloid precursor protein release via phosphatidyl inositol 3 kinase-dependent pathway. *FASEB J* 14, 1015–22.

Stern Y, Tang MX, Albert MS, et al (1997). Predicting time to nursing home care and death in individuals with Alzheimer disease. *JAMA* 277, 806–12.

Stewart R, Liolitsa D (1999). Type 2 diabetes mellitus, cognitive impairment and dementia. *Diabet Med* 16, 93–112.

Suo ZM, Fang CH, Crawford F, Mullan M (1997). Superoxide free radical and intracellular calcium mediate $A\beta_{1-42}$ induced endothelial toxicity. *Brain Res* 762, 144–52.

Thomas T, Thomas G, McLendon C, Sutton T, Mullan M (1996). β-Amyloid-mediated vasoactivity and vascular endothelial damage. *Nature* 380, 168–71.

Vassar R, Bennett BD, Babu-Khan S, et al (1999). Beta-secretase cleavage of Alzheimer's amyloid precursor protein by the transmembrane aspartic protease BACE. *Science* 286, 735–41.

Whitehouse PJ, Kittner B, Roessner M, et al (1998). Clinical trial designs for demonstrating disease-course-altering effects in dementia. *Alzheimer Dis Assoc Disord* **12**, 281–94.

Zarit SH, Todd PA, Zarit JM (1986). Subjective burden of husbands and wives as caregivers: a longitudinal study. *Gerontologist* **26**, 260–66.

Long-term care for the patient with dementia

9

Services for most people with dementia begin and, for many, end in the community. Institutional care is an important part of the total package of dementia care and some forms of institutional care prolong the period of time people with dementia can continue to live at home. By supporting carers and providing temporary respite and high quality dementia care, day hospitals and day centres can not only improve the quality of lives of sufferers' and their families but also prolong the period spent in the community. Hospitals themselves can provide respite care periods which allow the carer some time off whilst also being a period where concentrated attention to the patient's physical health can be and management of behavioural disturbances can be assessed. The provision of institutional care on a short-term basis to support community care is good practice in that it almost certainly improves quality of life and it is possible that the costs associated with provision of institutional care in the community might reduce the overall costs by limiting the time spent in long-term institutional care although evidence to support or refute this is hard to find. However, despite the value of community care and short-term institutional care, the provision of long-term institutional care is in many ways the most important element of a service package for people with dementia. Financially it is the most important element as the largest portion of direct costs for dementia are incurred by services for long-term care. In organisational terms it is the most important factor because long-term care replaces informal care with professional care. But most significantly, entry into long-term care means that families and carers have to come to terms with the last stages of a terminal condition and this point in the process heralds a period of grief and mourning for many relatives. For the patients themselves long-term care usually, although not always, means a loss of autonomy and, all too often, a loss of individuality. Good quality long-term care means many different things from good quality design through to good quality medical care. However, the best quality long-term care should also be attuned to the preservation of dignity and, as far as possible, autonomy of the demented person, and should also preserve the role of the family or principle care-giver.

Patterns of long-term care

The provision of, and reimbursement for, long-term care differs across countries. In the UK the elderly with mental health problems were, until relatively recently, cared for in large psychiatric hospitals. These institutions were often loathed by the local community and were themselves more often than not housed in the very same buildings as the Victorian Poor Law Workhouses. These institutions were the stuff of Dickens rather than modern dementia service provision and the wards were often of Nightingale design with a central nursing station and beds arrayed down either side of a long high room with windows providing light but no view as they were above the sight line of a seated person. Despite the best efforts of generations of staff, the provision of floral curtains and replacement of beds with easy chairs did little to render these appalling wards suitable for long-term care provision. Over recent years in the UK these institutions have all but disappeared and have been replaced by nursing homes, mostly run by for-profit companies or individuals, sometimes not-for-profit organisations and occasionally, but increasingly rarely, by the state through social services or health service budgets. A fierce debate has accompanied these changes, often focusing on costs and the sources of income available to fund placement. In the UK an attempt has been made to designate long-term care facilities as either providing skilled nursing and medical care or providing partially skilled or non-nursing care. It is immediately obvious that such a division is inherently unstable and to a certain extent arbitrary. It is, however, of real importance as the skilled nursing home care provision is funded by the National Health Service and therefore free at the point of use and not means-tested, whereas the residential care-only units are funded through social service budgets and means-tested. Given that the value of owner-occupied housing is incorporated into the means testing process (for those without spouses), large numbers of individuals have their estate consumed by long-term care.

In Canada a similar effect has arisen through a different process as demand for publicly funded institutions outstrips supply and is supplemented by private sector provision. In the USA the process reaches its natural conclusion as all long-term care is in the private sector. In Scandinavian countries and the Netherlands, by contrast, nursing homes in the community are a well established component of health care and the process of transfer from hospital to nursing home care has not occurred. As a consequence small, well supported, publicly funded nursing homes are a more common feature in these countries (Kane & Kane, 1976).

In addition to the nursing home many elderly people, some with dementia, live in supported housing – an intermediate form of care which is a compromise between support at home and full institutional care. In the UK these most often consist of purpose-built units of 20-100 fully independent units with some communal areas. The unit is supported by wardens who may be resident and are most often available 24 hours a day. In some units additional care is provided including group activities and meals. Such 'extra-care' facilities may be able to accommodate those with early dementia and some units have graded levels of accommodation which comprise supported housing, extra-care units and full nursing home provision, thus allowing a person with dementia to move thorough the system within a single building as the condition deteriorates. Accommodation in supported housing units such as these is often in high demand as the autonomy and privacy of the resident is preserved. For this reason relatives and other carers are often keen to secure such a placement for their relative with dementia although the units are most suitable for elderly frail people who are otherwise physically and mentally well. The advice that sheltered accommodation may not be suitable for those with dementia – even in the very early stages – can be a source of conflict. Nonetheless demand for such placements continues to rise. In the UK between 1950 and 1970 the age specific rate of residency in long-term nursing care facilities rose from 30 to 75 per 1000 (Evans, 1977). Approximately 5% of those over the age of 65 live in sheltered accommodation.

In the US an intermediate stage between home care support and nursing home care is provided by 'assisted living' units, the fastest-growing sector of long-term care provision (Kopetz et al, 2000). Residents in these units, like those in UK 'extra-care' sheltered accommodation units are younger, less impaired and suffer less behavioural disturbance than those in nursing home facilities. A similar situation exists in Sweden where 'Group Living' units are increasing in number and provide a level of care intermediate between that of community support and full nursing home care suitable for people with moderate dementia (Annerstedt, 1997).

Predicting entry into long-term care

The decision to place a relative in a long-stay facility is a difficult one and brings with it feelings of guilt and grief as well as more positive aspects such as relief from sleeplessness and respite from behavioural disturbance. The decision of when and whether to enter a nursing home can be a planned decision made by the relative in conjunction with the multi-disciplinary team or can occur as the result of a crisis or escalating problems at home. In a small study, Armstrong noted that a number of patients were placed in long-stay care around Christmas time (Armstrong, 2000) and certainly we have noted that for a variety of reasons holiday periods can be particularly stressful. The change in environment, visits from more distant relatives and the general stress and anxiety of such periods can put an extra strain on the carer and patient and result in a crisis admission. Further evidence that the placement process does not always follow the same set of criteria comes from a study of levels of dependency in a large set of nursing-homes where recently placed low-dependency residents were more likely to be self funded (as opposed to state funded) than the high-dependency residents, thus indicating that costs and resources also play a role in the decision as to when to enter long-term care (Challis et al, 2000).

Overall characteristics associated with long-term care entry include factors pertaining both to the patient and to the carer. As noted in chapter 7 male carers work differently to female carers and are more likely to access the full range of services on offer in contrast to female carers who tend to be more self- and family- reliant. Thus, having a wife may delay entry to a nursing home, while having a husband does so less (Heyman et al, 1997; Tomiak et al, 2000). Spouses make more committed carers than other relatives, the presence of whom increases likelihood of entry to a nursing home (Scott et al, 1997). Hope et al note that factors which predict institutionalisation in the medium-term are not the same as factors that precipitate entry to long-term care (Hope et al, 1998), the latter being active behavioural disturbances, in particular aggression. Nonetheless those patients most likely to require long-term care are those with behavioural disturbance, particularly sleeplessness and physical problems including immobility and incontinence (Armstrong, 2000; Hope et al,

1998). A series of systematic and longitudinal studies have found, not surprisingly, that more severely affected patients were admitted to nursing homes but in all cases it appears that it is function and not cognition that best predicts entry (Heyman et al, 1997; Juva et al, 1997; Scott et al, 1997; Severson et al, 1994; Steeman et al, 1997). In addition to carer factors and patient factors, the availability of other resources delays entry to long-term care (Bianchetti et al, 1995) although in some studies increased provision of services in turn increased the risk of admission to a nursing home probably because service provision reflects both availability and need (Nygaard & Albrektsen, 1992).

Case studies

While the data from surveys such as these is consistent – that more severe, more functionally impaired, older and more physically incapacitated patients are those most likely to be admitted to long-stay care, it can be difficult in practice to predict which individuals (from both the carer and patient perspective) will require nursing home placement. Two examples spring to mind:

Mrs A was referred to specialist services having recently transferred from another family doctor practice. She had not been seen by a doctor for many years. A remarkable story unfurled of a woman who

had been living alone and slowly deteriorating first in memory and then in function for more than five years., Her family were vary aware of her plight and arranged a rota so that one of them was with her much of the time and at a very minimum she had two visits a day. All her shopping, cooking and washing needs were provided by her family. She became increasingly disturbed at night and when neighbours complained members of the family took turns to sleep at her home. This became increasingly difficult for them – they all had families of their own – and the decision was made that Mrs A would go to live with one of her sons. Predictably she became more confused when she was moved and became sporadically incontinent. The response of her son was to keep her with him at all times. By the time the family sought help she was accompanying him to work, spending much of the day in the car and was moderately to severely demented with behavioural disturbance (wandering, sleeplessness, occasional vocalisations) as well as being incontinent. The provision of home care supports alleviated the situation somewhat but an extremely difficult situation for the family continued They continued to refuse long-term care placement.

Ms B on the other hand had mild dementia with no behavioural disturbance and only mild functional impairment. She lived with her friend of many decades who was functionally and cognitively intact. Both women had no family and were independent financially and after much thought requested nursing home placement. Their reasoning was that they could see that they would, over the forthcoming years become more dependent on the outside world rather than themselves. Although having only mild pathology between them their lives were already restricted by having to give up driving (for failing eyesight and general nervousness of driving). They felt they would prefer to become accustomed to group living in a caring environment whilst Ms B was able to understand and participate in the decision making.

Both Mrs A and Ms B provided exceptions to the rules predicting entry into nursing home. In fact such exceptions in our experience are not so uncommon and prove the delights of working with this group of patients and families. Clinicians and services caring for the elderly must be prepared to negotiate with each family as an individual case – for many entry into long-term care is a devastating and grief ridden event requiring sensitive support, while for others it can be a rational and life enhancing process.

Design and long-term care

Any design of a long term care facility is inevitably a compromise. On the one hand are the requirements of the patient – for the facility to be as like the normal home environment as possible, and on the other hand are the requirements that the facility be manageable – that residents can be seen and be safe. There is the compromise between normal living arrangements (with family, spouse or alone) and the arrangements necessary to provide care (in groups). There is the compromise, as always, between the desirable and the affordable. In the UK and most developed countries, long-term care facilities are provided both in purpose-built units and in adapted buildings. The latter often have the advantage of being most like the normal housing to which the residents are accustomed. London, for example, is peppered with nursing homes indistinguishable, apart from the sign outside, from the surrounding housing. These facilities, sometimes constructed from internal connections of adjacent housing, are instantly familiar to new residents. The room dimensions and décor are often identical to their own housing, recently vacated. However, these units are often barely suitable for the provision of long term care to demented patients. The room layout can promote isolation as individual residents spend much time in their own rooms with little scope to move around. Stairs can be narrow and steep and family houses rarely have rooms large enough to accommodate residents in a communal activity with comfort. Purpose built units on the other hand can offer large and varied communal rooms, easy access and safe environments. On the other hand they are all too often sterile, institutional and far removed from any environment that the residents have previously lived in.

There are, however, good examples of purpose built units and designed conversions of existing units that meet the compromise between utility and homeliness. It is this latter characteristic that is so important and the key to homeliness is empathy with the patient. In fact such empathy is not at all difficult to achieve. As Michael Manser, an architect with a particular interest in design for the infirm notes, "What the elderly and disabled probably wanted was what I wanted, but with more comfort, convenience and security... a location where life can be seen; an opportunity to see and mix with other age groups; a private place to live with your own possessions; and the choice to come and go. A place to live in, not one to wait in and die," (Manser, 1997 p411). One of us has a 90 year old relative in sheltered accommodation. Given a choice between a room overlooking a beautiful and well cared for garden or one on a busy and noisy road next to a shopping centre she had no hesitation in choosing the latter. As Manser notes, "Although

traditionally the idyllic image for the elderly and demented has been a sylvan scene, they are better stimulated by seeing a busy street scene – the busier the better."

Manser emphasises the need for long-stay care environments to resemble homes as much as possible despite the presence of protective surfaces, hand rails and easy-access doors. This idea has been called the 'homely' concept and is a good guiding principle for long-term care facility design. Alongside the 'homely' concept, long-stay facilities should 'make sense' – for example, corridors that have no purpose other than to be walked down, which people with dementia will do; circular designs will encourage demented people to walk around, surely something unlikely to improve orientation or well-being (Marshall, 1997). As Marshall notes, a corridor retains orientation only to the fire exit. Orientation can be aided by good design, constructive use of textures to differentiate a through-way from a bedroom (vinyl versus carpet for example) and different colour schemes for bathrooms, living rooms and bedrooms are both techniques used to good effect in some homes. Bedrooms need to have enough space to accommodate personal effects and residents should be encouraged to bring in their own furniture, mirrors and pictures even if this compromises the overall design of the building.

This personalisation of space should continue through to the staff. All too often the people in a home become the residents.

Not the same thing at all. Staff need to be helped and encouraged to find the person behind the resident, to learn something of their personal history, likes and dislikes and their family. All too often this is not the case and it can be difficult to identify a locus of responsibility for ensuring that staff not only care for but actually recognise the people in the home. As Cooper notes, "Old people admitted to long-term care in the homes are in a real sense displaced persons… biographical data that might be used to take advantage of former skills and interests are usually missing or fragmentary; the residents have 'lost their shadows." (Cooper, 1997). Good design as well as good staff morale and training could help preserve this individuality.

Dementia management in long-term care

A well-functioning long-stay facility will undertake regular medical and psychiatric review of residents. Health care issues in congregate dwellings include attention to group health (for example provision of influenza immunisation) as well as individual health. Much physical disability goes unrecognised in long-term care; large rates of undiagnosed hypotension were found in one study, for example (Butler et al, 1999), a problem that can increase morbidity and indeed mortality through falls. The abilities of individual residents should be known by the staff in order that maximisation of their cognitive and functional status can be achieved. Given that those in long-term care tend to be more impaired and more behaviourally disturbed there is considerable need for good management of behavioural disturbance. Often management itself becomes institutionalised and activities are applied to groups of residents en masse. However this can be ineffective and might in some residents even increase disturbance. Much behavioural disturbance in homes is in fact a direct consequence of some form of care activity on behalf of the staff (Keatinge et al, 2000). In a rare example of a controlled trial in this area Gerdner demonstrated that individualised music therapy sessions reduced agitation but that group classical music did not (Gerdner, 2000). In addition to appropriately individualised music therapy, physical activity regimes have been evaluated in this setting and have been shown to reduce deterioration in mobility and function (Lazowski et al, 1999). Other activities can include reminiscence therapy, visits to familiar places, artistic activities and so on. In general, however, the guiding principle should be individually designed programmes that make use of biographical information and carer discussions to generate a program most likely to appeal to pre-existing or latent abilities of the resident.

In addition to providing useful and enjoyable ways to pass time, activities can reduce behavioral disturbance. Inevitably, however, a high proportion of residents will display such disturbance regardless of stimulation. Active management of behavioural disturbance is therefore a priority in care homes and the principles outlined in Chapter 2 are as applicable in a nursing home as at home. In the USA and elsewhere some nursing homes have specialised in providing dementia care, known in the US as Special Care Units (SCUs). Alongside this development was the directive in the US (Omnibus Reconciliation Act of 1987; OBRA-87) that encouraged reduced use of physical restraints and anti-psychotic medication. Many assumed that if SCUs do indeed provide better care, then this would be manifested in lower use of psychotropic medications and physical restraints. However, this does not appear to be the case as shown in a survey of such homes in four states. Physical restraint was similar in SCUs but the use of antipsychotic medication was both common and actually higher in SCUs (52% of patients compared to 34-38% in the other units (Phillips et al, 2000)). It is difficult to know whether the higher use of psychotropic medication in SCUs reflects more efficacious treatment of BPSD, higher rates of BPSD or whether staff in SCUs have lower thresholds for using psychotropic medication. Good management of BPSD should not avoid the use of psychotropic medication – it is an effective and evidence-based treatment of a distressing set of symptoms – but there is no excuse for continued treatment beyond the necessary. Good practice within long-term care facilities would ensure regular review of all medication and audit of use over time in order to identify trends. In one such audit we found increased use of psychotropic medication correlated with decreased numbers of staff on duty at night for example (unpublished observation).

Summary

- Many but not all people with dementia spend some time in a long-term care facility.

- Patient features that predict entry to long term care include severity of functional impairment and behavioural disturbance as well as incontinence and physical immobility.

- Carer characteristics increasing likelihood of admission to a nursing home include being male.

- No two carer and patient dyads are alike, however, and some patients require early admission whist others strenuously defer admission

- The time of admission to a long-term care facility is difficult for the carer, the wider family and the patient themselves. This stage requires sensitive handling and support

- Good homes incorporate good design.

Good design is homely. The requirements of patients with dementia are not so dissimilar from yours.

* The needs of residents include regular medical review, individually tailored activities and appropriate management of behavioural disturbance.

References

Annerstedt L (1997). Group-living care: an alternative for the demented elderly. *Dement Geriatr Cogn Disord* 8, 136–42.

Armstrong M (2000). Factors affecting the decision to place a relative with dementia into residential care. *Nurs Stand* 14, 33–37.

Bianchetti A, Scuratti A, Zanetti O, et al (1995). Predictors of mortality and institutionalization in Alzheimer disease patients 1 year after discharge from an Alzheimer dementia unit. *Dementia* 6, 108–12.

Butler R, Fonseka, S Barclay L, et al (1999). The health of elderly residents in long term care institutions in New Zealand. *N Z Med J* 112, 427–29.

Challis D, Mozley CG, Sutcliffe C, et al (2000). Dependency in older people recently admitted to care homes. *Age Ageing* 29, 255–60.

Cooper B (1997). Principles of service provision in old age psychiatry, in *Psychiatry in the elderly*, 1 edn, R. Jacoby & C. Oppenheimer, eds., OUP, Oxford, 357–75.

Evans JG (1977). Current issues in the United Kingdom, in *Care of the Elderly: Meeting the challenge of dependency*, A. N. E. J. G. Exton-Smith, ed., Grune and Stratton, New York, 128–46.

Gerdner LA (2000). Effects of individualized versus classical 'relaxation' music on the frequency of agitation in elderly persons with Alzheimer's disease and related disorders. *Int Psychogeriatr* 12, 49–65.

Heyman A, Peterson B, Fillenbaum G, et al (1997). Predictors of time to institutionalization of patients with Alzheimer's disease: The CERAD experience 17. *Neurology* 48, 1304–9.

Hope T, Keene J, Gedling K, et al (1998). Predictors of institutionalization for people with dementia living at home with a carer. *Int J Geriatr Psychiatry* 13, 682–90.

Juva K, Makela M, Sulkava R, et al (1997). One-year risk of institutionalization in demented outpatients with caretaking relatives. *Int Psychogeriatr* 9, 175–82.

Kane RL, Kane RA (1976). *Long-term care in six countries* Department of Health, Eduaction and Welfare, Washington, DC.

Keatinge D, Scarfe C, Bellchambers H, et al (2000). The manifestation and nursing management of agitation in institutionalised residents with dementia. *Int J Nurs Pract* 6, 16–25.

Kopetz S, Steele CD, Brandt J, et al (2000). Characteristics and outcomes of dementia residents in an assisted living facility. *Int J Geriatr Psychiatry* 15, 586–93.

Lazowski DA, Ecclestone NA, Myers AM, et al (1999). A randomized outcome evaluation of group exercise programs in long-term care institutions. *J Gerontol A Biol Sci Med Sci* 54, M621–M628.

Manser M (1997). Better quality environments for people with dementia – design of environments, in *Psychiatry in the elderly*, 2nd edn, R. Jacoby & C. Oppenheimer, eds., OUP, Oxford, 410–20.

Marshall M (1997). Better quality environments for people with dementia – design and technology for people with dementia, in *Psychiatry in the elderly*, 2nd edn, R. Jacoby & C. Oppenheimer, eds., OUP, Oxford, 421–35.

Nygaard HA, Albrektsen G (1992). Risk factors for admission to a nursing home. A study of elderly people receiving home nursing. *Scand J Prim Health Care* 10, 128–33.

Phillips CD, Spry KM, Sloane PD, et al (2000). Use of physical restraints and psychotropic medications in Alzheimer special care units in nursing homes. *Am J Public Health* 90, 92–96.

Scott WK, Edwards KB, Davis DR, et al (1997). Risk of institutionalization among community long-term care clients with dementia. *Gerontologist* 37, 46–51.

Severson MA, Smith GE, Tangalos EG, et al (1994). Patterns and predictors of institutionalization in community- based dementia patients. *J Am Geriatr Soc* 42, 181–85.

Steeman E, Abraham IL, Godderis J (1997). Risk profiles for institutionalization in a cohort of elderly people with dementia or depression. *Arch Psychiatr Nurs* 11, 295–303.

Tomiak M, Berthelot JM, Guimond E, et al (2000). Factors associated with nursing-home entry for elders in Manitoba, Canada. *J Gerontol A Biol Sci Med Sci* 55, M279–M287.

Assessment scales and management of Alzheimer's disease

10

The core of all assessment in dementia care is careful enquiry and attentive listening, and there is no substitute for a clinical interview by a trained doctor, nurse, psychologist or occupational therapist. However, having acknowledged this, there is a special and important role for the use of formal scales in dementia assessment. The reason for this is not entirely clear – assessment scales are used in all medical conditions in research but only rarely elsewhere in ordinary clinical practice. Probably the reasons are multiple – partly because the patients themselves are less able to describe the symptoms, partly because the symptoms are context-sensitive (better functional ability in own home than in somewhere less familiar for example), and partly because the symptoms are, to a certain extent, subjective. Some types of symptoms lend themselves better to formal assessment using scales than others. Cognitive symptoms in particular lend themselves so readily to assessment using scales that for many clinicians it is easy to forget that the widespread use of scales in clinical practice is a relatively recent phenomenon. Assessing other aspects of the life and symptoms of a person with dementia is more challenging. There are no very useful quality of life scales and it could be argued that attempting to perform such an assessment using a scale alone is taking the reductionist approach to assessment one step too far.

One advantage of using scales is that of reliability both between assessors and over the course of time. Another is the reductionism itself: although this has to be balanced by a clinical and 'holistic' assessment, the provision of a number allows measurement of change and ready comparison of the patient to others and to population norms. One further, almost hidden, advantage of scales is that they can act as a prompt to full clinical assessment. The incorporation of a set of assessment scales into clinical practice can encourage, for example, full and pro-active assessment of behaviour rather than relying on a reactive assessment following carer complaint.

When planning an assessment using scales it is important to balance practicality with scientific rigour. Scales formulated for use in research may not always be suitable for use in clinical practice. One example of this that has caused particular problems is that of cognitive tests. Invariably clinical trials of cholinesterase inhibitors have used the ADAS-cog as a primary outcome measure, in the mild to moderate stages of Alzheimer's disease. The scale is comprehensive enough to give an assessment of a wide range of cognitive abilities, was specifically designed for assessment of cognitive function, and is highly reliable with excellent validity. However, it takes approximately 45 minutes with a trained

rater. Few clinical services have the resources to contemplate such an assessment in routine clinical practice. On the other hand the Mini-Mental State Examination (MMSE) is a relatively non-comprehensive measure of cognitive function that was designed for screening for cognitive impairment rather than actual assessment. In truth the variability between assessments in the MMSE makes it a poor measure of cognitive function. However, it is quick (10 minutes or less) to perform and therefore less stressful to patients and easily incorporated into clinical practice. Moreover it is almost certainly the most widely used scale measuring any aspect of dementia, it has extensive normative data in the elderly available and must be familiar to almost all of us working in the clinical field of dementia care. Therefore when choosing a scale to measure cognition in response to drug treatments in clinical practice the choice is between the excellent scale used as the primary outcome measure in clinical trials that takes longer than the time available for full assessment of the patient, and a less than perfect scale that is easily performed. The choice is obvious for most and we imagine few services use the ADAS-cog.

In this chapter we have included a selection of scales which we hope might be useful in clinical practice. Most scales, including these, were derived with research in mind and all have received at least some form of validity and reliability testing. Most but not all of these scales are useful for research – many are indeed used in clinical studies but the needs of research are such that the choice of a particular scale for a particular project carries quite different considerations to choosing a scale for clinical practice. We increasingly use scales, including some of those below, in our clinical practice and for use in this context the scale should be relatively quick to perform and should require minimal training to conduct it and to interpret the results. The use of self-rating scales by carers complements interviewer-assessment. Preferably the scale will be used with ease by all members of the multi-disciplinary team.

Assessment of cognition

Three levels of assessment can be distinguished with respect to cognition. Comprehensive measures of cognitive ability; assessment or screening in secondary care, and screening in primary care. Comprehensive measures of cognitive ability are best performed using scales all the way from the ADAS-cog through to detailed neuro-psychometric testing taking many hours. We include the ADAS-cog as it may have some role in memory clinics and other specialised units. For other purposes the MMSE is most suitable in secondary care although there are limitations to its use as noted above. These limitations are not always appreciated. For example, the UK expert group the National Institute for Clinical Excellence (NICE), a government established body,

approved the use of cholinesterase inhibitors for AD only for those with MMSE scores between 24 and 12. However, clearly it is possible to have dementia, and to be recognised as having dementia, with a score above 24. Equally a score of below 12 is a poor measure of severity. As in all tests the MMSE should be used to complement and not replace clinical assessment. The MMSE is a 30-point scale with 24 being the cut-off for screening for dementia and takes 10 minutes or less to perform with only a minimal amount of training necessary. Even the MMSE is probably too time-consuming for routine screening purposes in primary care where 10 minutes might represent the full extent of the interview. For opportunistic and routine screening in primary care the Abbreviated Mental Test Score (AMTS) can be used to good effect. An alternative and surprisingly informative test is the clock-drawing test that takes only a few minutes to perform. The clock drawing test can also be used as a fairly coarse measure of deterioration. Research and treatment units dealing with severe dementia will find the severe impairment battery very useful and user-friendly.

Assessment of behavioural and psychological symptoms of dementia

Assessment of behaviour has only fairly recently come under the scrutiny of the advocates of scales. While there are many scales that measure different aspects of behaviour, there is one scale in particular that has been used to good effect in both clinical practice and clinical research. The Neuro-psychiatric Inventory (NPI) is a brief clinician-conducted interview with a carer that takes 10 minutes and rates the extent, severity and frequency of a variety of behaviours. It is an excellent and deservedly popular scale. Assessing depression in dementia is particularly difficult and the NPI can usefully be complemented by the Cornell Depression in Dementia Scale (CDDS). Other scales are available for agitation, aggression, and so forth but a more comprehensive scale often used in clinical trials is the BEHAVE-AD, a highly reliable but more time-consuming measure.

Assessment of function

We have included three scales of assessment of function. This was a somewhat arbitrary and personal choice as there are many scales in this area. The Interview for Deterioration in Daily Living Activities in Dementia (IDDD) is a fairly complex measure which relies upon an informant interview. It measures over 30 distinct activities on a three point scale and takes less than 15 minutes although as with all carer-based interviews the questions can prompt more detailed responses from the interviewee resulting in an extended interview. The IDDD has been used in clinical trials as

has the Bristol Activities of Daily Living scale (B-ADL). This latter scale is particularly useful as it is carer-rated and experienced carers can complete the assessment whilst the clinician is assessing cognitive performance in the patient, for example. This has the dual effect of making the process more practicable in clinical practice and also distracting the carer, thereby reducing their understandable desire to help the patient. Similarly, the disability assessment in dementia (DAD) is a 40-question scale designed to be completed by interviewing the carer regarding instrumental and self-care activities performed during the previous two weeks.

Global assessment and carer assessment

It was probably the FDA decision to require a global deterioration measure in assessing efficacy of anti-dementia drugs that has resulted in the huge importance attached to this aspect of assessment. We include details of two overlapping assessment measures. The Clinicians' Global Impression of Change and its variants are used in almost all clinical trials and are essentially a formalisation of the clinicians' assessment of change based upon their assessment of the patient together and in some cases with the carers' assessment. The Functional Assessment Staging (FAST) and the Geriatric Depression Scale (GDS) are a combined assessment measure that attempt the same method of assessment but have the advantage of providing very brief descriptions of severity that are matched to the patient's state. In clinical practice, especially where the same patient may be assessed by many raters, and where those raters may be from different disciplines, then the GDS/FAST is particularly useful if a global measure is needed. For follow-up of treatment over a year or more, the Clinical Dementia Rating (CDR) scale is quite useful since it explores in a semi-structured way six complementary domains of cognition and function.

Assessment of carer stress is of two broad types – assessment of the carer's mental state using generic stress or depression scales, or assessment of the carer's perceptions of the amount of time spent caring or the burden they are suffering from. We have included one scale we find useful, the Burden Interview, a self-report scale completed within the interview.

Mini-Mental State Examination (MMSE)

Max score	*Score*	
		ORIENTATION
5	( )	What is the (year) (season) (date) (month) (day)?
5	( )	Where are we: (state) (county) (town) (hospital) (floor)?
		REGISTRATION
3	( )	Name 3 objects: (1 second to say each). Then ask the patient all three after you have said them.
		Give 1 point for each correct answer. Then repeat them until the patient learns all 3. Count trials and record.
		Number of Trials _____
		ATTENTION AND CALCULATION
5	( )	Serial 7's. 1 point for each correct. Stop after 5 answers. If the patient refuses, spell "world" backwards.
		RECALL
3	( )	Ask for 3 objects repeated above. Give 1 point for each correct.
		LANGUAGE
9	( )	Name a pencil; name a watch. (2 points)
		Repeat the following: "No ifs, ands or buts." (1 point)
		Follow a three stage command: "Take this paper in your right hand, fold it in half, and put it on the floor." (3 points)
		Read and obey the following: "Close your eyes." (1 point)

Write a sentence. (1 point)

Copy a design. (1 point)

Total Score _____   Assess level of
                       consciousness
                       along a continuum

_____
Alert   Drowsy   Stupor   Coma

Mental Test Score (MTS)/Abbreviated Mental Test Score

ORIGINAL TEST ITEMS

	Score
Name	*0/1*
Age	*0/1*
Time (to nearest hour)	*0/1*
Time of day	*0/1*
Name and address for five minutes recall; this should be repeated by the patient to ensure it has been heard correctly.	
Mr John Brown	*0/1/2*
42 West Street	*0/1/2*
Gateshead	*0/1*
Day of week	*0/1*
Date (correct day of month)	*0/1*
Month	*0/1*
Year	*0/1*
Place: Type of place (i.e. Hospital)	*0/1*
Name of Hospital	*0/1*
Name of ward	*0/1*
Name of town	*0/1*
Recognition of two persons (doctor, nurse, etc.)	*0/1/2*
Date of birth (day and month sufficient)	*0/1*
Place of birth (town)	*0/1*
School attended	*0/1*
Former occupation	*0/1*

Name of wife, sib or next of kin	*0/1*
Date of First World War (year sufficient)	*0/1*
Date of Second World War (date sufficient)	*0/1*
Name of present Monarch	*0/1*
Name of present Prime Minister	*0/1*
Months of year backwards	*0/1/2*
Count 1–20	*0/1/2*
Count 20–1	*0/1/2*
Total	*(34)*

ABBREVIATED MENTAL TEST SCORE

1. *Age*
2. *Time (to nearest hour)*
3. *Address for recall at end of test – this should be repeated by the patient to ensure it has been heard correctly: 42 West Street*
4. *Year*
5. *Name of hospital*
6. *Recognition of two persons (doctor, nurse, . . .)*
7. *Date of birth*
8. *Year of First World War*
9. *Name of present Monarch*
10. *Count backwards 20–1*

(each question scores one mark)

Source: Hopkinson M (1972) Evaluation of a mental test score for assessment of mental impairment in the elderly. *Age and Ageing* 1: 233–8. By kind permission of Oxford University Press.

Alzheimer's Disease Assessment Scale (ADAS) – Cognitive and Non-Cognitive Sections (ADAS-Cog, ADAS-Non-Cog)

Cognitive Items

1. Spoken language ability _____
2. Comprehension of spoken language _____
3. Recall of test instructions _____
4. Word-finding difficulty _____
5. Following commands _____
6. Naming: objects, fingers _____

High:	1	2	3	4	Fingers: Thumb
Medium:	1	2	3	4	Pinky Index
Low:	1	2	3	4	Middle Ring

7. Constructions: drawing _____
   Figures correct: 1   2   3   4
   Closing in: Yes _____ No _____
8. Ideational praxis _____
   Step correct:
   1   2   3   4   5
9. Orientation _____
   Day ___ Year ___ Person ___ Time of day ___
   Date ___ Month ___ Season ___ Place ___
10. Word recall: mean error score _____
11. Word recognition: mean error score _____
    Cognition total _____

Non-cognitive Items (all rated by examiner)

12. Tearful _____
13. Appears/reports depressed mood _____
14. Concentration, distractibility _____
15. Uncooperative to testing _____
16. Delusions _____
17. Hallucinations _____
18. Pacing _____
19. Increased motor activity _____
20. Tremors _____
21. Increase/decrease appetite _____
    Noncognition total _____

Total Scores

Cognitive behavior _____
Non-cognitive behavior _____
Word recall _____
Word recognition _____
   Total _____

Rating: x = not assessed
   0 = not present
   1 = very mild
   2 = mild
   3 = moderate
   4 = moderately severe
   5 = severe

*Spoken language – quality of speech **not** quantity.*
*Comprehension – do **not** include responses to commands.*
Do not include finger or object naming.
Score   0–5 steps correct
   1–4 steps correct
   2–3 steps correct
   3–2 steps correct
   4–1 steps correct
   5 – cannot do one step correct

Name fingers of dominant hand and high/medium/low frequency objects.
0 = all correct; one finger incorrect and/or one object incorrect
1 = two–three fingers and/or two objects incorrect
2 = two or more fingers and three–five objects incorrect
3 = three or more fingers and six–seven objects incorrect
4 = three or more fingers and eight–nine objects incorrect

Ability to copy circle, two overlapping rectangles, rhombus and cube.

5 components in sending self a letter
1 = difficulty or failure to perform one component
2 = difficulty and/or failure to perform two components
3 = difficulty and/or failure to perform three components
4 = difficulty and/or failure to perform four components
5 = difficulty and/or failure to perform five components

Date, month, year, day of week, season, time of day, place and person.

Noncognitive behavior is evaluated over preceding week to interview.

American Journal of Psychiatry, Vol. 141, pp. 1356–64, 1984. Copyright 1984, the American Psychiatric Association. Reprinted by permission.

Clock Drawing Test

A priori criteria for evaluating clock drawings
(10 = best and 1 = worst)

10–6. *Drawing of Clock Face with Circle and Numbers is Generally Intact*

10. *Hands are in correct position (i.e. hour hand approaching 3 o'clock)*

9. *Slight errors in placement of the hands*

8. *More noticeable errors in the placement of hour and minute hands*

7. *Placement of hands is significantly off course*

6. *Inappropriate use of clock hands (i.e. use of digital display or circling of numbers despite repeated instructions)*

5–1. *Drawing of Clock Face with Circle and Numbers is Not Intact*

5. *Crowding of numbers at one end of the clock or reversal of numbers. Hands may still be present in some fashion.*

4. *Further distortion of number sequence. Integrity of clock face is now gone (i.e. numbers missing or placed at outside of the boundaries of the clock face).*

3. *Numbers and clock face no longer obviously connected in the drawing. Hands are not present.*

2. *Drawing reveals some evidence of instructions being received but only a vague representation of a clock.*

1. *Either no attempt or an uninterpretable effort is made.*

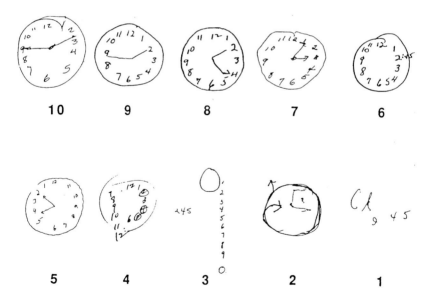

Samples of clock drawings from Alzheimer patients with evaluations of best (10) to worst (1).

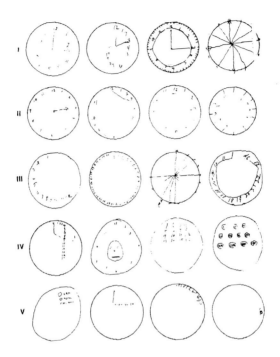

Clinical examples of clock errors

Classification of clock errors
I   *Visuospatial*
   (a)   *Mildly impaired spacing of times*
   (b)   *Draws times outside circle*
   (c)   *Turns page while writing numbers so that some numbers appear upside down*
   (d)   *Draws in lines (spokes) to orient spacing*
II   *Errors in denoting the time as 3 o'clock*
   (a)   *Omits minute hand*
   (b)   *Draws a single line from 12 to 3*
   (c)   *Writes the words '3 o'clock'*
   (d)   *Writes the number 3 again*
   (e)   *Circles or underlines 3*
   (f)   *Unable to indicate 3 o'clock*
III *Visuospatial*
   (a)   *Moderately impaired spacing of times (so that 3 o'clock cannot be accurately denoted)*

(b)   Omits numbers
Preservation
(a)   Repeats the circle
(b)   Continues on past 12 to 13, 14, 15, etc.
Right–Left reversal – numbers drawn counterclockwise
Dygraphia – unable to write numbers accurately
IV   *Severely disorganized spacing*
(a)   Confuses 'time' – writes in minutes, times of day, months or seasons
(b)   Draws a picture of human face on the clock
(c)   Writes the word 'clock'
V   *Unable to make any reasonable attempt at a clock*
(excludes severe depression or other psychotic state)

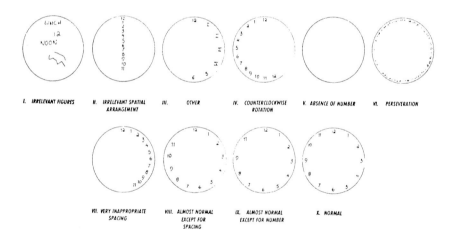

The 10 clock patterns

Sources: Sunderland T, Hill JL, Mellow AM, Lawlor BA, Gundersheimer J, Newhouse PA, Grafman JH (1989) Clock drawing in Alzheimer's disease; and Wolf-Klein GR, Silverstone FA, Levy AP, Brod MS, Breuer J (1989) Screening for Alzheimer's disease by clock drawing, *Journal of American Geriatrics Society.* Vol. 37, no. 8. pp. 725–9 and 730–4, respectively; also Brodaty H, Moore CM (1997) The Clock Drawing Test for dementia of the Alzheimer's type: a comparison of three scoring methods in a memory disorders clinic; and Shulman K, Shedlecksky R, Silver I (1986) The challenge of time. Clock drawing and cognitive function in the elderly, *International Journal of Geriatric Psychiatry.* Vol. 12, pp. 619–27 and Vol. 1, pp. 135–40, respectively (Copyright John Wiley & Sons Limited. Reproduced with permission).

Severe Impairment Battery (SIB)

Reference   Saxton J, McGonigle-Gibson K, Swihart A, Miller M, Boller F (1990) Assessment of severely impaired patients: description and validation of a new neuropsychological test battery. *Psychological Assessment* 2: 298–303

Time taken   30–40 minutes (reviewer's estimate)
Rating   by trained interviewer

Main indications
Assessment of cognitive function, particularly in severe dementia.

Commentary
The Severe Impairment Battery (SIB) has the strength of assessing cognitive function in patients with moderate to severe dementia. Items are single words or one-step commands combined with gestures. Nine areas are assessed (see below), and the score is between 0 and 100. It appears to change. Panisset et al (1994)

examined 69 patients with severe dementia using the SIB and found it to be a helpful neuropsychological measure in people with severe dementia.

Additional references
Albert M, Cohen C (1992) The Test for Severe Impairment, an instrument for the assessment of patients with severe cognitive dysfunction. *Journal of American Geriatric Society* **40**: 449–53.
Panisset M, Roudier M, Saxon J et al (1994) Severe Impairment Battery: a neuropsychological battery for severely impaired patients. *Archives of Neurology* **51**: 41–5.

Severe Impairment Battery Domains

Domain	Questions
Orientation	*Name*
	Place (town)
	Time (month and time of day)
Attention	*Digit span*
	Counting to visual and auditory stimuli
Language	*Auditory and reading comprehension*
	Verbal fluency (food and months of the year)
	Naming from description, pictures of objects, objects, colors and forms
	Repetition
	Reading
	Writing
	Copying of written material
Praxis	*How to use a cup, a spoon*
Visuospatial	*Discrimination of colors and forms*
Construction	*Spontaneous drawing, copying and tracing a figure*
Memory	*Immediate short- and long-term recall for examiner's name, objects, colors, forms and a short sentence*
Orientation to name	*When the patient's name is called from behind*
Social interaction	*Shaking hands, following general direction*

Source: Panisset M, Roudier M, Saxton J et al (1994) Severe Impairment Battery: a neuropsychological battery for severely impaired patients. *Archives of Neurology* **51**: 41–5.

BEHAVE-AD

Part 1: Symptomatology

Assessment Interval: Specify: _____ wks.

Total Score: _____

a. Paranoid and Delusional Ideation

1. "People are Stealing Things" Delusion

0 = Not present.

1 = Delusion that people are hiding objects.

2 = Delusion that people are coming into the home and hiding objects or stealing objects.

3 = Talking and listening to people coming into the home.

2. "One's House is Not One's Home" Delusion

0 = Not present.

1 = Conviction that the place in which one is residing is not one's home (e.g. packing to go home; complaints, while at home, of "take me home").

2 = Attempt to leave domiciliary to go home.

3 = Violence in response to attempts to forcibly restrict exit.

3. "Spouse (or Other Caregiver) is an Imposter" Delusion

0 = Not present.

1 = Conviction that spouse (or other caregiver) is an imposter.

2 = Anger toward spouse (or other caregiver) for being an imposter.

3 = Violence towards spouse (or other caregiver) for being an imposter.

4. "Delusion of Abandonment" (e.g. to an Institution)

0 = Not present.

1 = Suspicion of caregiver plotting abandonment or institutionalization (e.g. on telephone).

2 = Accusation of a conspiracy to abandon or institutionalize.

3 = Accusation of impending or immediate desertion or institutionalization.

5. "Delusion of Infidelity"

0 = Not present.

1 = Conviction that spouse and/or children and/or other caregivers are unfaithful.

2 = Anger toward spouse, relative, or other caregiver for infidelity.

3 = Violence toward spouse, relative, or other caregiver for supposed infidelity.

6. "Suspiciousness/Paranoia" (other than above)

0 = Not present.

1 = Suspicious (e.g. hiding objects that he/she later may be unable to locate).

2 = Paranoid (i.e. fixed conviction with respect to suspicions and/or anger as a result of suspicions).

3 = Violence as a result of suspicions.

Unspecified?

Describe

7. Delusions (other than above)

0 = Not present.

1 = Delusional.

2 = Verbal or emotional manifestations as a result of delusions.

3 = Physical actions or violence as a result of delusions.

Unspecified?

Describe

b. Hallucinations

8. Visual Hallucinations

0 = Not present.

1 = Vague: not clearly defined.

2 = Clearly defined hallucinations of objects or persons (e.g. sees other people at the table).

3 = Verbal or physical actions or emotional responses to the hallucinations.

9. Auditory Hallucinations

0 = Not present.

1 = Vague: not clearly defined.

2 = Clearly defined hallucinations of words or phrases.

3 = Verbal or physical actions or emotional response to the hallucinations.

10. Olfactory Hallucinations

0 = Not present.

1 = Vague: not clearly defined.

2 = Clearly defined.

3 = Verbal or physical actions or emotional responses to the hallucinations.

11. Haptic Hallucinations

0 = Not present.

1 = Vague: not clearly defined.

2 = Clearly defined.

3 = Verbal or physical actions or emotional responses to the hallucinations.

12. Other Hallucinations

0 = Not present.

1 = Vague: not clearly defined.

2 = Clearly defined.

3 = Verbal or physical actions or emotional responses to the hallucinations.

Unspecified?

Describe

c. Activity Disturbances

13. Wandering: Away From Home or Caregiver

0 = Not present.

1 = Somewhat, but not sufficient to necessitate restraint.

2 = Sufficient to require restraint.

3 = Verbal or physical actions or emotional responses to attempts to prevent wandering.

14. Purposeless Activity (Cognitive Abulia)

0 = Not present.

1 = Repetitive, purposeless activity (e.g. opening and closing pocketbook, packing and unpacking clothing, repeatedly putting on and removing clothing, opening and closing drawers, insistent repeating of demands or questions).

2 = Pacing or other purposeless activity sufficient to require restraint.

3 = Abrasions or physical harm resulting from purposeless activity.

15. Inappropriate Activity

0 = Not present.

1 = Inappropriate activities (e.g. storing and hiding objects in inappropriate places, such as throwing clothing in wastebasket or putting empty plates in the oven; inappropriate sexual behavior, such as inappropriate exposure).

2 = Present and sufficient to require restraint.

3 = Present, sufficient to require restraint, and accompanied by anger or violence when restraint is used.

d. Aggressiveness

16. Verbal Outbursts

0 = Not present.

1 = Present (including unaccustomed use of foul or abusive language).

2 = Present and accompanied by anger.

3 = Present, accompanied by anger, and clearly directed at other persons.

17. Physical Threats and/or Violence

0 = Not present.

1 = Threatening behavior.

2 = Physical violence.

3 = Physical violence accompanied by vehemence.

18. Agitation (other than above)

0 = Not present.

1 = Present.

2 = Present with emotional component.

3 = Present with emotional and physical component.

Unspecified?

Describe

e. Diurnal Rhythm Disturbances

19. Day/Night Disturbance

0 = Not present.

1 = Repetitive wakenings during night.

2 = 50% to 75% of former sleep cycle at night.

3 = Complete disturbance of diurnal rhythm (i.e. less than 50% of former sleep cycle at night).

f. *Affective Disturbance*
20. Tearfulness
0 = Not present.
1 = Present.
2 = Present and accompanied by clear affective component.
3 = Present and accompanied by affective and physical component (e.g. "wrings hands" or other gestures).

21. Depressed Mood: Other
0 = Not present.
1 = Present (e.g. occasional statement "I wish I were dead," without clear affective concomitants).
2 = Present with clear concomitants (e.g. thoughts of death).
3 = Present with emotional and physical component (e.g. suicide gestures).
Unspecified?
Describe

g. *Anxieties and Phobias*
22. Anxiety Regarding Upcoming Events (Godot Syndrome)
0 = Not present.
1 = Present: Repeated queries and/or other activities regarding upcoming appointments and/or events.
2 = Present and disturbing to caregivers.
3 = Present and intolerable to caregivers.

23. Other Anxieties
0 = Not present.
1 = Present.
2 = Present and disturbing to caregivers.

3 = Present and intolerable to caregivers.
Unspecified?
Describe

24. Fear of Being Left Alone
0 = Not present.
1 = Present: Vocalized fear of being alone.
2 = Vocalized and sufficient to require specific action on part of caregiver.
3 = Vocalized and sufficient to require patient to be accompanied at all times.

25. Other Phobias
0 = Not present.
1 = Present.
2 = Present and of sufficient magnitude to require specific action on part of caregiver.
3 = Present and sufficient to prevent patient activities.
Unspecified?
Describe

Part 2: Global Rating
With respect to the above symptoms, they are of sufficient magnitude as to be:
0 = Not at all troubling to the caregiver or dangerous to the patient.
1 = Mildly troubling to the caregiver or dangerous to the patient.
2 = Moderately troubling to the caregiver or dangerous to the patient.
3 = Severely troubling or intolerable to the caregiver or dangerous to the patient.

Neuropsychiatric Inventory (NPI)

Reference   Cummings JL, Mega M, Gray K, Rosenberg-Thompson S, Carusi DA, Gornbein J (1994)
The Neuropsychiatric Inventory: comprehensive assessment of psychopathology in dementia.
Neurology 44: 2308–14

Time taken   10 minutes

Rating   by clinician in interview with a carer

Main indications

The Neuropsychiatric Inventory (NPI) evaluates a wider range of psychopathology than comparable instruments, and may help distinguish between different causes of dementia; it also records severity and frequency separately.

Commentary

The NPI is a relatively brief interview assessing 10 behavioural disturbances: delusions; hallucinations; dysphoria; anxiety; agitation/aggression; euphoria; disinhibition; irritability/ lability; apathy; and aberrant motor behavior. It uses a screening strategy to cut down the length of time the instrument takes to administer, but it obviously takes longer if replies are positive. It is scored from 1 to 144. Severity and frequency are independently assessed. The authors reported on 40 caregivers, and content and concurrent validity and inter-rater and test/retest reliability were assessed. Some 45 assessments were used for the inter-rater reliability and 20 for

test/retest reliability. Concurrent validity was found to be satisfactory using a panel of appropriated experts; concurrent reliability was determined by comparing the NPI subscale with subscales of the BEHAVE-AD (page 75) and the Hamilton Depression Rating Scale (page 4). Highly significant correlations were found. A high level of internal consistency (0.88) was found using a Cronbach's coefficient. Inter-rater reliability revealed agreement in over 90 ratings, and test/retest reliability (a second interview within 3 weeks) was very highly significant. A training pack and further information is available from the author.

Address for correspondence

JL Cummings
Neurobehavior Unit
Psychiatry Service (116F)
West Los Angeles, VAMC
11301 Wilshire Blvd
Los Angeles
CA 90073
USA

Neuropsychiatric Inventory (NPI)

Description of the NPI

The NPI consists of 12 behavioral areas

Delusions	*Apathy*
Hallucinations	*Disinhibition*
Agitation	*Irritability*
Depression	*Aberrant motor behavior*
Anxiety	*Night-time behaviors*
Euphoria	*Appetite and eating disorders*

Frequency is rated as
1. *Occasionally – less than once per week*
2. *Often – about once per week*
3. *Frequently – several times a week but less than every day*
4. *Very frequently – daily or essentially continuously present*

Severity is rated as
1. *Mild – produce little distress in the patient*
2. *Moderate – more disturbing to the patient but can be redirected by the caregiver*
3. *Severe – very disturbing to the patient and difficult to redirect*

Distress is scored as
0 — no distress
1 — minimal
2 — mild
3 — moderate
4 — moderately severe
5 — very severe or extreme

For each domain there are 4 scores. Frequency, severity, total (frequency × severity) and caregiver distress. The total possible score is 144 (i.e. A maximum of 4 in the frequency rating × 3 in the severity rating × 12 remaining domains). This relates to changes, usually over the 4 weeks prior to completion.

Source: Cummings JL, Mega M, Gray K, Rosenberg-Thompson S, Carusi DA, Gornbein J (1994) The Neuropsychiatric inventory: comprehensive assessment of psychopathology in dementia. *Neurology* 44: 2308–14.

Cornell Scale for Depression in Dementia

A. **Mood-Related Signs**
1. *Anxiety*
    anxious expression, ruminations, worrying
2. *Sadness*
    sad expression, sad voice, tearfulness
3. *Lack of reactivity to pleasant events*
4. *Irritability*
    easily annoyed, short tempered

B. **Behavioral Disturbance**
5. *Agitation*
    restlessness, handwringing, hairpulling
6. *Retardation*
    slow movements, slow speech, slow reactions
7. *Multiple physical complaints*
    (score 0 if GI symptoms only)
8. *Loss of interest*
    less involved in usual activities (score only if change occurred acutely, i.e. in less than 1 month)

C. **Physical Signs**
9. *Appetite loss*
    eating less than usual
10. *Weight loss*
    (score 2 if greater than 5 lb in 1 month)

11. *Lack of energy*
    fatigues easily, unable to sustain activities (score only if change occurred acutely, i.e. in less than 1 month)

D. **Cyclic Functions**
12. *Diurnal variation of mood*
    symptoms worse in the morning
13. *Difficulty falling asleep*
    later than usual for this individual
14. *Multiple awakenings during sleep*
15. *Early morning awakening*
    earlier than usual for this individual

E. **Ideational Disturbance**
16. *Suicide*
    feels life is not worth living, has suicidal wishes, or makes suicide attempt
17. *Poor self-esteem*
    self-blame, self-depreciation, feelings of failure
18. *Pessimism*
    anticipation of the worst
19. *Mood-congruent delusions*
    delusions of poverty, illness, or loss

Rating:
a = Unable to evaluate; 0 = Absent; 1 = Mild or intermittent; 2 = Severe
All based on week prior to interview

Interview for Deterioration in Daily Living Activities in Dementia (IDDD)

Reference   Teunisse S, Derix MMA (1991) Measuring functional disability in community dwelling dementia patients: development of a questionnaire. *Tijdschrift voor Gerontologie en Geriatrie* **22**: 53–9

Time taken   15 minutes (reviewer's estimate)

Rating   by interview with main caregiver

Main indications

To assess activities of daily living in dementia.

Commentary

The scale covers 33 activities such as washing, dressing, and eating as well as more complex activities such as shopping, writing and answering the telephone, tasks performed equally by men and women (earlier scales of activities of daily living tended to rely more heavily on female-dominated and less complex tasks). Both the initiative to perform activities and the performance itself were evaluated. There was high internal consistency (alpha = 0.94) and two groups of items were discriminated: those related to self-care activity and those to more complex tasks. Functioning of the patient is examined in a structured verbal interview with the carer. The scoring is rated on a three-point scale: 1 where help is almost never needed or there has been no change, 2 where help is sometimes needed or when help is needed more often than previously, and 3 when help is almost always needed or help is needed much more than previously. The scoring is carried out by referring to behaviour in the last month, comparing it with how it was before the onset of the dementia. After a negative response the questioner is asked to check that the behaviour is unchanged compared with what it was like previously, and after positive response questions are asked: "is the help really necessary?" "what happens if you don't help?" and "do you have to help more often than before?"

The original paper rated functional disability along with cognitive impairment (measured by the CAMCOG), behavioural disturbances [measured by the GIP (page 124)] and carer burden [measured by an instrument related to the Zarit Burden Interview (page 239)]. Inter-relationships were found in 30 mild to moderately impaired patients with dementia. Functional disability was strongly related to cognitive deterioration and behavioural disturbances, and moderately related to burden experienced by carers. Since 1991, the IDDD has been translated into several languages and a paper-and-pencil version has been used in the measurement of treatment effects.

Additional reference

Teunisse S, Derix MMA, van Crevel H (1991) Assessing the severity of dementia: patient and caregiver. *Archives of Neurology* **48**: 274–7.

Address for correspondence

S Teunisse
Psychology Department
William Guild Building
King's College
University of Aberdeen
Aberdeen AB24 2UB
UK

Interview for Deterioration in Daily Living Activities in Dementia (IDDD)

1. *Do you have to tell her that she should wash herself (take the initiative to wash herself; not only washing of hands or face, but also washing of whole body)?*   1   2   3   8   9
2. *Do you have to assist her in washing (finding face cloth, soap; soaping and rinsing of the body)?*   1   2   3   8   9
3. *Do you have to tell her that she should dry herself (take the initiative to dry herself, for example looking or fetching for the towel)?*   1   2   3   8   9
4. *Do you have to assist her in drying (drying individual body-parts)?*   1   2   3   8   9
5. *Do you have to tell her that she should dress herself (take the initiative to dress herself, for example walking to the wardrobe)?*   1   2   3   8   9
6. *Do you have to assist her in dressing herself (putting on individual clothes in right order)?*   1   2   3   8   9
7. *Do you have to assist her in doing up her shoes, using zippers or buttons?*   1   2   3   8   9
8. *Do you have to tell her that she should brush her teeth or comb her hair?*   1   2   3   8   9
9. *Do you have to assist her in brushing her teeth?*   1   2   3   8   9
10. *Do you have to assist her in combing her hair?*   1   2   3   8   9
11. *Do you have to tell her that she should eat (take the initiative to eat; in case eating is elicited by others, it should be asked if she would take the initiative spontaneously)?*   1   2   3   8   9
12. *Do you have to assist her in preparing a slice of bread?*   1   2   3   8   9
13. *Do you have to assist her in carving meat, potatoes?*   1   2   3   8   9
14. *Do you have to assist her in drinking or eating?*   1   2   3   8   9
15. *Do you have to tell her that she should use the lavatory (take the initiative to go to the lavatory when necessary)*   1   2   3   8   9
16. *Do you have to assist her in using the toilet (undressing herself, using toilet, using closet paper)?*   1   2   3   8   9
17. *Do you have to assist her in finding her way in the house (finding different rooms)?*   1   2   3   8   9
18. *Do you have to assist her in finding her way in familiar neighbourhood outside the house?*   1   2   3   8   9
19. *Does she – as often as before – take the initiative shopping (take the initiative to figure out what is needed)?*   1   2   3   8   9
20. *Do you have to assist her in shopping (finding her way in the shops; getting goods in needed quantity)?*   1   2   3   8   9
21. *Do you – or the shop-assistant – have to tell her that she should pay?*   1   2   3   8   9
22. *Do you – or the shop-assistant – have to assist her in paying (knowing how much she should pay and how much should be reimbursed)?*   1   2   3   8   9
23. *Is she – as often as before – interested in newspaper, book or post?*   1   2   3   8   9
24. *Do you have to assist her in reading (understanding written language)?*   1   2   3   8   9
25. *Do you have to assist her in writing a letter or card, or completing a form (writing of more than one sentence)?*   1   2   3   8   9
26. *Does she – as often as before – start a conversation with others?*   1   2   3   8   9
27. *Do you have to assist her in expressing herself verbally?*   1   2   3   8   9

28.	Does she – as often as before – pay attention to conversation by other people?	1	2	3	8	9
29.	Do you have to assist her in understanding spoken language?	1	2	3	8	9
30.	Does she – as often as before – take the initiative to use the phone (both answering the phone and calling someone)?	1	2	3	8	9
31.	Do you have to assist her in using the phone (both answering the phone and calling someone)?	1	2	3	8	9
32.	Do you have to assist her in finding things in the house?	1	2	3	8	9
33.	Do you have to tell her to put out gas or coffee machine?	1	2	3	8	9

Rating:
1 = (nearly) no help needed/no change in help needed
2 = sometimes help needed/help more often needed
3 = (nearly) always help needed/help much more often needed
8 = no evaluation possible
9 = not applicable

Reproduced (with permission from the American Medical Association) from Teunisse S et al. (1991) Assessing the severity of dementia: patient and caregiver. *Archives of Neurology*, **48**: 274–7. Copyright 1991. American Medical Association.

Bristol Activities of Daily Living Scale

Reference   Bucks RS, Ashworth DL, Wilcock GK, Siegfried K (1996) Assessment of activities of daily living in dementia: development of the Bristol Activities of Daily Living Scale. *Age and Ageing* **25**: 113–20

Time taken   15 minutes (reviewer's estimate)
Rating   by carer

Main indications
Assessment of activities of daily living in patients with dementia either in the community or on clinical research trial.

Commentary
The scale was designed specifically for use in patients with dementia, and consists of 20 daily living abilities. Face validity was measured by way of carer agreement that the items were important, construct validity was confirmed by principal components analysis, concurrent validity by assessment with observed performance and good test/rest reliability. Three phases in the design of the

scale were described. Anyone designing a scale should read this to serve as a model of clarity.

Additional reference
Patterson MB, Mack JL, Neundorfer MM et al (1992) Assessment of functional ability in Alzheimer's disease: a review and preliminary report on the Cleveland Scale for Activities of Daily Living. *Alzheimer Disease and Associated Disorders* **6**: 145–63.

Address for correspondence
GK Wilcock
Department of Care of the Elderly
Frenchay Hospital
Bristol BS16 1LE
UK

Bristol Activities of Daily Living Scale

1. Food
a. Selects and prepares food as required [ ]
b. Able to prepare food if ingredients set out [ ]
c. Can prepare food if prompted step by step [ ]
d. Unable to prepare food even with prompting and supervision [ ]
e. Not applicable [ ]

2. Eating
a. Eats appropriately using correct cutlery [ ]
b. Eats appropriately if food made manageable and/or uses spoon [ ]
c. Uses fingers to eat food [ ]
d. Needs to be fed [ ]
e. Not applicable [ ]

3. Drink
a. Selects and prepares drinks as required [ ]
b. Can prepare drinks if ingredients left available [ ]
c. Can prepare drinks if prompted step by step [ ]
d. Unable to make a drink even with prompting and supervision [ ]
e. Not applicable [ ]

4. Drinking
a. Drinks appropriately [ ]
b. Drinks appropriately with aids, beaker/straw etc. [ ]
c. Does not drink appropriately even with aids but attempts to [ ]
d. Has to have drinks administered (fed) [ ]
e. Not applicable [ ]

5. Dressing
a. Selects appropriate clothing and dresses self [ ]
b. Puts clothes on in wrong order and/or back to front and/or dirty clothing [ ]
c. Unable to dress self but moves limbs to assist [ ]
d. Unable to assist and requires total dressing [ ]
e. Not applicable [ ]

6. Hygiene
a. Washes regularly and independently [ ]
b. Can wash self if given soap, flannel, towel, etc. [ ]
c. Can wash self if prompted and supervised [ ]
d. Unable to wash self and needs full assistance [ ]
e. Not applicable [ ]

7. Teeth
a. Cleans own teeth/dentures regularly and independently [ ]
b. Cleans teeth/dentures if given appropriate items [ ]
c. Requires some assistance, toothpaste on brush, brush to mouth, etc. [ ]
d. Full assistance given [ ]
e. Not applicable [ ]

8. Bath/shower
a. Bathes regularly and independently [ ]
b. Needs bath to be drawn/shower turned on but washes independently [ ]
c. Needs supervision and prompting to wash [ ]
d. Totally dependent, needs full assistance [ ]
e. Not applicable [ ]

9. Toilet/commode
a. Uses toilet appropriately when required [ ]
b. Needs to be taken to the toilet and given assistance [ ]
c. Incontinent of urine or faeces [ ]
d. Incontinent of urine and faeces [ ]
e. Not applicable [ ]

10. Transfers
a. Can get in/out of chair unaided [ ]
b. Can get into a chair but needs help to get out [ ]
c. Needs help getting in and out of a chair [ ]
d. Totally dependent on being put into and lifted from chair [ ]
e. Not applicable [ ]

11. Mobility
a. Walks independently [ ]
b. Walks with assistance, i.e. furniture, arm for support [ ]
c. Uses aids to mobilize, i.e. frame, sticks etc. [ ]
d. Unable to walk [ ]
e. Not applicable [ ]

12. Orientation – time
a. Fully orientated to time/day/date etc. [ ]

b. *Unaware of time/day etc. but seems*
unconcerned [ ]
c. *Repeatedly asks the time/day/date* [ ]
d. *Mixes up night and day* [ ]
e. *Not applicable* [ ]
13. Orientation – space
a. *Fully orientated to surroundings* [ ]
b. *Orientated to familiar surroundings only* [ ]
c. *Gets lost in home, needs reminding*
where bathroom is, etc. [ ]
d. *Does not recognize home as own and*
attempts to leave [ ]
e. *Not applicable* [ ]

14. Communication
a. *Able to hold appropriate conversation* [ ]
b. *Shows understanding and attempts to*
respond verbally with gestures [ ]
c. *Can make self understood but difficulty*
understanding others [ ]
d. *Does not respond to or communicate*
with others [ ]
e. *Not applicable* [ ]

15. Telephone
a. *Uses telephone appropriately, including*
obtaining correct number [ ]
b. *Uses telephone if number given verbally*
/visually or predialled [ ]
c. *Answers telephone but does not make*
calls [ ]
d. *Unable/unwilling to use telephone at all* [ ]
e. *Not applicable* [ ]

16. Housework/gardening
a. *Able to do housework/gardening to*
previous standard [ ]
b. *Able to do housework/gardening but*
not to previous standard [ ]
c. *Limited participation even with a lot of*
supervision [ ]
d. *Unwilling/unable to participate in*
previous activities [ ]

e. *Not applicable* [ ]
17. Shopping
a. *Shops to previous standard* [ ]
b. *Only able to shop for 1 or 2 items with*
or without a list [ ]
c. *Unable to shop alone, but participates*
when accompanied [ ]
d. *Unable to participate in shopping even when*
accompanied [ ]
e. *Not applicable* [ ]

18. Finances
a. *Responsible for own finances at*
previous level [ ]
b. *Unable to write cheque but can sign*
name and recognizes money values [ ]
c. *Can sign name but unable to recognize money*
values [ ]
d. *Unable to sign name or recognize*
money values [ ]
e. *Not applicable* [ ]

19. Games/hobbies
a. *Participates in pastimes/activities to*
previous standard [ ]
b. *Participates but needs instruction/*
supervision [ ]
c. *Reluctant to join in, very slow, needs coaxing* [ ]
d. *No longer able or willing to join in* [ ]
e. *Not applicable* [ ]

20. Transport
a. *Able to drive, cycle or use public*
transport independently [ ]
b. *Unable to drive but uses public*
transport or bike etc. [ ]
c. *Unable to use public transport alone* [ ]
d. *Unable or unwilling to use transport*
even when accompanied [ ]
e. *Not applicable* [ ]

Rating:
Tick only 1 box per activity. Answer with respect to last 2 weeks
Score: a 5 0, b 5 1, c 5 2, d 5 3, e 5 0

Reprinted from Bucks RS, Ashworth DL, Wilcock GK, Siegfried K (1996) Assessment of activities of daily living in dementia: development of the Bristol Activities of Daily Living Scale. *Age and Ageing*, **25**: 113–20. By kind permission of Oxford University Press.

Geriatric Depression Scale (GDS)

Choose the best answer for how you felt the past week

1. *Are you basically satisfied with your life?*
2. *Have you dropped many of your activities and interests?*
3. *Do you feel that your life is empty?*
4. *Do you often get bored?*
5. *Are you hopeful about the future?*
6. *Are you bothered by thoughts you can't get out of your head?*
7. *Are you in good spirits most of the time?*
8. *Are you afraid that something bad is going to happen to you?*
9. *Do you feel happy most of the time?*
10. *Do you often feel helpless?*
11. *Do you often get restless and fidgety?*
12. *Do you prefer to stay at home, rather than going out and doing new things?*
13. *Do you frequently worry about the future?*
14. *Do you feel you have more problems with memory than most?*
15. *Do you think it is wonderful to be alive now?*
16. *Do you often feel downhearted and blue?*
17. *Do you feel pretty worthless the way you are now?*
18. *Do you worry a lot about the past?*
19. *Do you find life very exciting?*
20. *Is it hard for you to get started on new projects?*
21. *Do you feel full of energy?*
22. *Do you feel that your situation is hopeless?*
23. *Do you think that most people are better off than you are?*
24. *Do you frequently get upset over little things?*
25. *Do you frequently feel like crying?*
26. *Do you have trouble concentrating?*
27. *Do you enjoy getting up in the morning?*
28. *Do you prefer to avoid social gatherings?*
29. *Is it easy for you to make decisions?*
30. *Is your mind as clear as it used to be?*

Code answers as Yes or No

Score 1 for Yes on: 2–4,6,8,10–14,16–18,20,22–26,28
Score 1 for No on: 1,5,7,9,15,19,21,27,29,30

0–10 = Not depressed
11–20 = Mild depression
21–30 = Severe depression
GDS 15: 1,2,3,4,7,8,9,10,12,14,15,17,21,22,23 (cut-off of 5/6 indicates depression)
GDS 10: 1,2,3,8,9,10,14,21,22,23
GDS 4: 1,3,8,9 (cut-off of 1/2 indicates depression)

Reprinted from *Journal of Psychiatric Research*, Vol. 17, Yesavage JA, Brink TL, Rose TL, Lum O, Huang V, Adey M, Leirer O, Development and validation of a geriatric depression scale: a preliminary report, 1983, with permission from Elsevier Science.

Functional Assessment Staging (FAST)

Yes	*Months[1]*	*No.*		
____	_____	____	*1.*	No difficulties, either subjectively or objectively.
____	_____	____	*2.*	Complains of forgetting location of objects; subjective work difficulties.
____	_____	____	*3.*	Decrease job functioning evident to coworkers; difficulty in traveling to new locations.
____	_____	____	*4.*	Decreased ability to perform complex tasks (e.g., planning dinner for guests; handling finances; marketing)
____	_____	____	*5.*	Requires assistance in choosing proper clothing.
____	_____	____	*6a.*	Difficulty putting clothing on properly.
____	_____	____	*6b.*	Unable to bathe properly; may develop fear of bathing.
____	_____	____	*6c.*	Inability to handle mechanics of toileting (i.e., forgets to flush, doesn't wipe properly).
____	_____	____	*6d.*	Urinary incontinence.
____	_____	____	*6e.*	Fecal incontinence.
____	_____	____	*7a.*	Ability to speak limited (1 to 5 words a day).
____	_____	____	*7b.*	All intelligible vocabulary lost.
____	_____	____	*7c.*	Nonambulatory.
____	_____	____	*7d.*	Unable to sit up independently.
____	_____	____	*7e.*	Unable to smile.
____	_____	____	*7f.*	Unable to hold head up.

TESTER: _____   *COMMENTS:* _____

Note: *Functional staging score = Highest ordinal value. [1]Number of months FAST stage deficit has been noted.*

Clinical Dementia Rating (CDR)

	Impairment				
	None *0*	*Questionable* *0.5*	*Mild* *1*	*Moderate* *2*	*Severe* *3*
Memory	No memory loss or slight inconstant forgetfulness	Consistent slight forgetfulness; partial recollection of events; "benign" forgetfulness	Moderate memory loss; more marked for recent events; defect interferes with everyday activities	Severe memory loss; only highly learned material retained; new material rapidly lost	Severe memory loss; only fragments remain
Orientation	Fully oriented	Fully oriented except for slight difficulty with time relationships	Moderate difficulty with time relationships; oriented for place at examination; may have geographic disorientation elsewhere	Severe difficulty with time relationships; usually disoriented to time, often to place	Oriented to person only
Judgment and Problem Solving	Solves everyday problems and handles business and financial affairs well; judgment good in relation to past performance	Slight impairment in solving problems, similarities, and differences	Moderate difficulty in handling problems, similarities, and differences; social judgment usually maintained	Severely impaired in handling problems, similarities, and differences; social judgment usually impaired	Unable to make judgments or solve problems
Community Affairs	Independent function at usual level in job, shopping, and volunteer and social groups	Slight impairment in these activities	Unable to function independently at these activities although may still be engaged in some; appears normal to casual inspection	No pretense of independent function outside home Appears well enough to be taken to functions outside a family home	No pretense of independent function outside home Appears too ill to be taken to functions outside a family home
Home and Hobbies	Life at home, hobbies, and intellectual interests well maintained	Life at home, hobbies, and intellectual interests slightly impaired	Mild but definite impairment of function at home; more difficult chores abandoned; more complicated hobbies and interests abandoned	Only simple chores preserved; very restricted interests, poorly maintained	No significant function in home
Personal Care	Fully capable of self-care		Needs prompting	Requires assistance in dressing, hygiene, keeping of personal effects	Requires much help with personal care; frequent incontinence

Rating:
Score only as decline from previous usual level due to cognitive loss, not impairment due to other factors

Burden Interview

Reference   Zarit SH, Reever KE, Bach-Petersen J (1980) Relatives of the impaired elderly: correlates of feeling of burden. *The Gerontologist* **20**: 649–55

Time taken   25 minutes (reviewer's estimate)
Rating   by self-report during an assessment interview

Main indications
Assessment of the feelings of burden of caregivers in caring for an older person with dementia.

Commentary
Twenty-nine patients with senile dementia and their caregivers were interviewed, and the Burden Interview was compared with measures of cognitive function (Khan Mental Status Questionnaire; Khan et al, 1960), a measure of mental state (Jacobs et al, 1977), a measure of the Memory and Problems Checklist and activities of daily living as assessed by scales described by Lawton (1971). The amount of burden assessed was found to be less when more visits were made by carers to the patient with dementia, and severity of behavioural problems was not associated with higher levels of burden. The paper was one of the earlier studies to underscore the importance of providing support to caregivers in the community care of older people with dementia.

Additional references
Jacobs JW, Bernhard JR, Delgado A et al (1977) Screening for organic mental syndromes in the medically ill. *Annals of Internal Medicine* **86**: 40–6.

Khan RL, Goldfarb AI, Pollack J et al (1960) A brief objective measure for the determination of mental status of the aged. *American Journal of Psychiatry* **117**: 326–8.

Lawton MP (1971) The functional assessment of elderly people. *Journal of the American Geriatrics Society* **19**: 465–80.

Address for correspondence
Steve Zarit
Gerontology Center
College of Health and Human Development
Pennsylvania State University
105 Henderson Building South
University Park
PA 16802–6500
USA

Burden Interview

1. I feel resentful of other relatives who could but who do not do things for my spouse.
2. I feel that my spouse makes requests which I perceive to be over and above what s/he needs.
3. Because of my involvement with my spouse, I don't have enough time for myself.
4. I feel stressed between trying to give to my spouse as well as to other family responsibilities, job, etc.
5. I feel embarrassed over my spouse's behavior.
6. I feel guilty about my interactions with my spouse.
7. I feel that I don't do as much for my spouse as I could or should.
8. I feel angry about my interactions with my spouse.
9. I feel that in the past, I haven't done as much for my spouse as I could have or should have.
10. I feel nervous or depressed about my interactions with my spouse.
11. I feel that my spouse currently affects my relationships with other family members and friends in a negative way.
12. I feel resentful about my interactions with my spouse.
13. I am afraid of what the future holds for my spouse.
14. I feel pleased about my interactions with my spouse.
15. It's painful to watch my spouse age.
16. I feel useful in my interactions with my spouse.
17. I feel my spouse is dependent.
18. I feel strained in my interactions with my spouse.
19. I feel that my health has suffered because of my involvement with my spouse.
20. I feel that I am contributing to the well-being of my spouse.
21. I feel that the present situation with my spouse doesn't allow me as much privacy as I'd like.
22. I feel that my social life has suffered because of my involvement with my spouse.
23. I wish that my spouse and I had a better relationship.
24. I feel that my spouse doesn't appreciate what I do for him/her as much as I would like.
25. I feel uncomfortable when I have friends over.
26. I feel that my spouse tries to manipulate me.
27. I feel that my spouse seems to expect me to take care of him/her as if I were the only one he/she could depend on.
28. I feel that I don't have enough money to support my spouse in addition to the rest of our expenses.
29. I feel that I would like to be able to provide more money to support my spouse than I am able to now.

Clinician's Global Impression of Change (CGIC)

Alzheimer's Disease Cooperative Study

A Multicenter Evaluation of New Treatment Efficacy Instruments for AD

Clinical Trials

Clinical Global Impression of Change – Summary Sheet

Baseline Visit

Center Name	Subject Number	Subject Initials	Examiner Initials	Examination Date
	I N			Month Day Year

1. Order of Administration
   □ Subject first, Informant second
   □ Informant first, Subject second

2. Time of day interview started:

   ☐☐☐☐ (24 hour clock)

3. The following sources of information were used in completing this assessment (check all that apply)
   □ Interview/examination of subject
   □ Interview of Informant
   □ Information on neuropsychological test performance
   □ General information derived from a staff conference about subject
   □ Other, please specify: _____

ADCS–CLINICAL GLOBAL IMPRESSION OF CHANGE WORKSHEETS

Part 1–BASELINE CGIC Evaluation for both Subject and Informant

SUBJECT MUST BE INTERVIEWED FIRST

Subject Initials: _____ Subject ID: IN-___-___ Examiner Initials: _____ Date: _____

Time of day interview started: _____ (24 hour clock)

Brief Instructions: See instruction sheet. Use this form to record baseline information for assessing change at a later date. Information can be obtained from all relevant sources, including subject, informant, and staff members. A brief clinical assessment of mental state should be made. No particular format or order is suggested for the interview.

Area	Probes	Notes
Relevant history	recent relevant clinical events, illnesses?	Subject
		Informant
Observation/ Evaluation	appearance	Subject
		Informant
MENTAL/COGNITIVE STATE (Structured exam, if used: _____)		
Arousal/ Alertness/ Attention/ Concentration	confusion/clarity excitement/reactivity state of consciousness	Subject
		Informant

Area	Probes	Notes
Orientation	time place person	Subject
		Informant
Memory	registration recall long term/remote recall for past events	Subject
		Informant
Language/ Speech	fluency/ expressive language receptive language comprehension paraphasia/word finding naming, amount repetition follows directions	Subject
		Informant
Praxis	constructional ability ideational praxis ideomotor/imitation	Subject
		Informant

Area	Probes	Notes
Judgment/ Problem solving/ Insight	patient's behaviour in situations requiring judgment	Subject
		Informant
BEHAVIOUR		
Thought content	organization appropriateness	Subject
		Informant
Hallucinations/ Delusions/ Illusions	auditory/visual misperceptions systematized/developed	Subject
		Informant
Behaviour/Mood	affect/lability unusual/bizarre uninhibited motivation/energy wandering/getting lost agitation/aggression hostility depression-related anxiety-related appropriateness cooperativeness	Subject
		Informant

Area	Probes	Notes	
Sleep/Appetite	sleep disorder insomnia (type?) nocturnal activity hyper-, hyposomnia appetite/weight change	Subject	
		Informant	
Neurological/ Psychomotor activity	overall motor activity postural/gait movement disorder unusual motor behaviour daily patterns	Subject	
		Informant	
FUNCTIONING			
Basic and complex Instrumental/ functional ability	mobility hygiene/grooming dressing self-feeding shopping household chores/hobbies finances driving	Subject	
		Informant	
Social function	participation in: social interactions community activities independence helplessness	Subject	
		Informant	

Notes, comments, summary statement:

Information from other sources:

The following sources of information were used in completing this form:

– Interview/examination of subject

– Interview of informant. Describe relationship to subject: _____

– Information on neuropsychological test performance

– General information derived from a staff conference about the subject

– Other: _____

DISABILITY ASSESSMENT FOR DEMENTIA (DAD)

Authors:	L Gauthier and I Gélinas
Collaborators:	M McIntyre, S Gauthier,
	H Laberge and S Wood
	Dauphinee

Introduction

The literature as well as consultations with health care professionals and caregivers clearly indicates the need for a disability measure designed specifically for community-dwelling individuals with dementia of the Alzheimer type (DAT). Such an instrument is essential to help clinicians and caregivers make decisions regarding the choice of suitable interventions and to monitor disease progression. In addition, as a research tool, it could be used to describe the functional characteristics of populations with DAT, the course of the disease and also as an outcome variable in intervention studies and clinical trials. The Disability Assessment for Dementia (DAD) Scale was developed in an attempt to fulfill these needs.

Objectives of the DAD

The objectives of the DAD Scale are to quantitatively measure functional abilities in activities of daily living (ADL) in individuals with cognitive impairments such as dementia and to help delineate areas of cognitive deficits which may impair performance in ADL. Basic and instrumental activities of daily living are examined in relation to executive skills to permit identification of the problematic areas. The primary aim is to have a standardized, valid, reliable and sensitive measure of functional disability in DAT and other dementias. Another objective is to obtain a French and English instrument which is short and easy to administer.

Target population

The DAD Scale is intended specifically for the assessment of disability in community residing individuals with cognitive deficits such as DAT and other dementias. This tool has not been designed to meet the specific needs of populations with physical disabilities (neuro-muscular deficits). In cases where an individual will present both cognitive and physical deficits which may impair function in ADL, this tool should not be used exclusively but rather in conjunction with another assessment of ADL designed for physical disabilities.

DISABILITY ASSESSMENT FOR DEMENTIA (DAD)

Name:		File No:	
Date:	MMS:	GDS:	DAD:
Respondent:		Relationship:	
Specify all motor and sensory disorders:			
Rater:		Time:	

During the past two weeks, did (name) _____, without help or reminder

HYGIENE   SCORING: YES = 1   NO = 0   N/A = Not Applicable

Item	Initiation	Planning & Organization	Effective Performance
HYGIENE			
Undertake to wash himself/herself or to take a bath or a shower		■	■
Undertake to brush his/her teeth or care for his/her dentures		■	■
Decide to care for his/her hair (wash and comb)		■	■
Prepare the water, towels, and soap for washing, taking a bath or a shower	■		■
Wash and dry completely all parts of his/her body safely	■	■	
Brush his/her teeth or care for his/her dentures appropriately	■	■	
Care for his/her hair (wash and comb)	■	■	
DRESSING			
Undertake to dress himself/herself		■	■
Choose appropriate clothing (with regard to the occasion, neatness, the weather and color combination)	■		■
Dress himself/herself in the appropriate order (undergarments, pant/dress, shoes)	■		■
Dress himself/herself completely	■	■	
Undress himself/herself completely	■	■	
CONTINENCE			
Decide to use the toilet at appropriate times		■	■
Use the toilet without "accidents"	■	■	
EATING			
Decide that he/she needs to eat		■	■
Choose appropriate utensils and seasonings when eating	■	■	
Eat his/her meals at a normal pace and with appropriate manners	■	■	
MEAL PREPARATION			
Undertake to prepare a light meal or snack for himself/herself		■	■
Adequately plan a light meal or snack (ingredients, cookware)	■		■
Prepare or cook a light meal or a snack safely	■	■	
TELEPHONING			
Attempt to telephone someone at a suitable time		■	■
Find and dial a telephone number correctly	■		■
Carry out an appropriate telephone conversation	■	■	
Write and convey a telephone message adequately	■	■	

During the past two weeks, did (name) _____, without help or reminder

	Initiation	Planning & Organization	Effective Performance

GOING ON AN OUTING   SCORING: YES=1   NO=0   N/A=Not Applicable

	Initiation	Planning & Organization	Effective Performance
Undertake to go out (walk, visit, shop) at an appropriate time	■		
Adequately organize an outing with respect to transportation, keys, destination, weather, necessary money, shopping list		■	
Go out and reach a familiar destination without getting lost			■
Safely take the adequate mode of transportation (car, bus, taxi)			■
Return from the store with the appropriate items			■

FINANCE AND CORRESPONDENCE

Show an interest in his/her finances and written correspondence	■		
Organize his/her finance to pay his/her bills (cheques, bankbook, bills)		■	
Adequately organize his/her correspondence with respect to stationery, address, stamps		■	
Handle adequately his/her money (make change)			■

MEDICATIONS

Decide to take his/her medications at the correct time	■		
Take his/her medications as prescribed (according to the right dosage)			■

LEISURE AND HOUSEWORK

Show an interest in leisure activity(ies)	■		
Take an interest in household chores that he/she used to perform in the past	■		
Plan and organize adequately household chores that he/she used to perform in the past		■	
Complete household chores adequately as he/she used to perform in the past			■
Stay safely at home by himself/herself when needed			■

Comments:

SUB TOTAL/#applicable items	/	/	/
DAD TOTAL/#applicable items	/		
DAD TOTAL in %			

Appendix

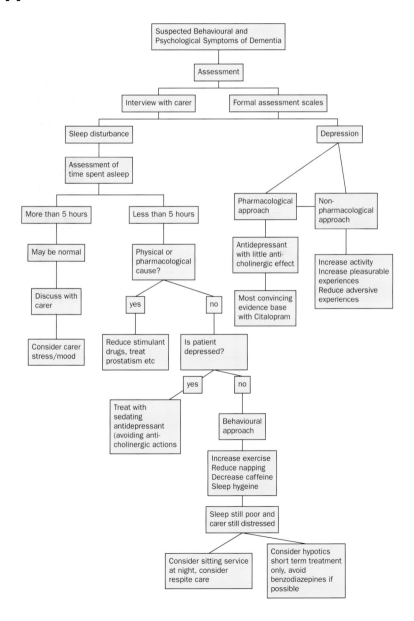

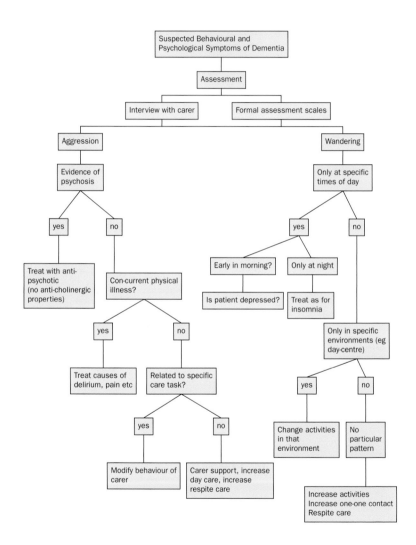

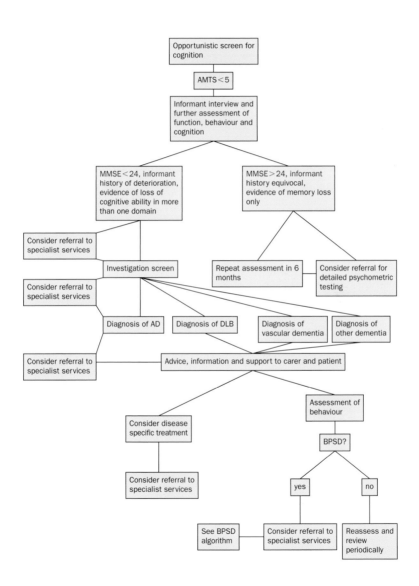

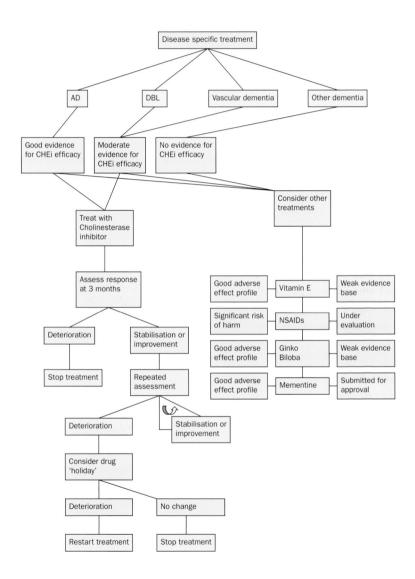

Recommended reading

Clinical diagnosis and management of Alzheimer's disease. Serge Gauthier (ed.) Martin Dunitz, London, 2nd revised edition 2001.
Written primarily by and for clinicians, this book reviews the diagnosis, natural history, and management of Alzheimer's disease from the medical, community resources and institutional point of views.

Concepts of Alzheimer Disease. Biological, clinical, and cultural perspectives. Peter J Whitehouse, Konrad Maurer, Jesse F Ballenger (eds). The Johns Hopkins University Press, Baltimore & London, 2000.
This book offers a historical perspective on Alzheimer's disease, an insight into its impact on the person and society, and future perspectives.

Diagnosis and management of dementia. A manual for memory disorders teams. Gordon K Wilcock, Romola S Bucks, Kenneth Rockwood (eds) Oxford University Press, 1999.
A systematic approach to setting up a memory clinic.

Health Economics of Dementia. Anders Wimo, Bengt Jönsson, Göran Karlsson, Bengt Winblad (eds) John Wiley & Sons, Chichester, 1998.
This is the current main reference on the costs of dementia, including quality of life issues and ethics of pharmacoeconomics.

Late-stage dementia care. A basic guide. Christine R Kovach. Taylor & Francis, 1997.
Detailed and practical advice for management of dementia in later stages.

The Dementias. John H Growdon, Martin N. Rossor (eds) Butterworth Heinemann, Boston, 1998.
Systematic reviews of the degenerative dementias with emphasis on pathphysiology.

Understanding dementia. A primer of diagnosis and management. Kenneth Rockwood, Chris MacKnight.
Potterfield Press Ltd, Halifax, 2001.
A step by step approach to diagnosis and early management of dementia for primary care practitioners.

Department of Social Policy and Social Work
University of Oxford
Barnett House
32 Wellington Square
Oxford OX1 2ER
England